Communion With God

And

Community With Man

Rodney Allan Tilley

Printed in the United States of America
First Printing 2020

ISBN #97986662713895

Cover Design: Kindle Direct Publishing
Publisher: Kindle Direct Publishing

Author contact:
Rodney Allan Tilley
Email: randjtilley@gmail.com
This book can also be found as an eBook on Kindle eBooks.

Dedication

This book is dedicated to my father, Robert Tilley, and my mother, Delcie Tilley who through their example and teaching showed me personally how to be in Communion with God and in Community with Man. They taught me how to live and love as Christ did, and set a high standard of behavior to emulate and to follow. I am eternally grateful for their love and compassion that they showed me as their son. They were examples that have proven to be true from birth to the grave. I love them both.

CONTENTS

Communion with God, Community with Man

Have you ever felt lost, confused, and just unsure of what life was all about, well, I have and sometimes still am. In my years in university, I studied in the fields of psychology and religion and I read the conflicting systems of thought and tried a variety of psychological therapies. I was looking for answers from those that apparently did not have any and so I experimented with the psychological healing of mind and body and tried sane and some unbelievably insane applications of seeking wellness of the soul. My professor, for example, in one "off the wall" therapy, told me that I must learn to release the non-dynamic orgones, or energy particles, that plague my body and soul, and so I sat under an orgone blanket of wool, steel wool, and cotton. It was covered in shiny aluminum foil, and I was told I would feel the orgones leaving my body. However, all I felt was an itch from the rash I caught from the interaction of steel wool and fiberglass.

Another university teacher, the one who contracted a four year marriage with a new incoming freshman each term, (He was totally self-absorbed), informed us that in our development as a child, some of us did not physically crawl enough and now as an adult we must crawl around to reconnect those neurons that were not mature. I crawled around the house for a month, until I felt I was a turtle looking for a home. I decided I wanted to come out of my shell, so I started to walk upright again, and move up the food chain one more notch.

Others said, you must release your primal man, and I did so by yelling at the top of my voice with a primal scream. My throat got sore and my neighbors complained of the excess noise coming from my apartment. I read books on self-actualization and dream interpretation and came to understand that pizza at night and dream interpretation can be totally confusing and conflicting.

Psychologist Carl Rogers said I must, "Become a Person," and Dr. Carl Jung said I must learn to "know and express myself through my collective unconsciousness." Sigmund Freud told us to look into our past subliminal consciousness and understand that sex controlled our every thought in our every conscious ego driven mania. I have been actualized, socialized, homogenized, and individualized. I have been taken through the therapy modalities such CBT, REBT, ABC, and all the other letters of the alphabet. It seems that everybody who had a new thought and who could write a sentence, wrote a book about their favorite theory. For a want-to-be hippie like me, I was compelled to try and sort out this massive material of diverse thinking, to which I failed miserably.

However, the Christian world of theological thinking was not much better. One church denomination would tell me one compelling fact, and another one would tell me something completely opposite. They told me that the only way to heaven was through them and that their theological facts were directly from the Bible. I was told, "You must say these words," and do these acts, and not say these words. I was told to speak in an unknown tongue, but only in private, but sometimes in public, but only to really show I had it, whatever it was. I must repent, and repent again, but not too much. I must profess my faith in words, both understood and in words that no one could understand. I was told of works and of faith, of love and of justice. What was right and what was wrong and when it was right. I was as confused with both sides of the coin and I read and reread the Bible. After some time in thought and prayer, and through heavy arguments, some things began to change.

As I got older, I began to lay aside the fluff and get to the meat of the matter both from a religious-theological perspective and from a social-psychological one as well. I found that life can be seen in a much simpler application and platform of religious thought. I thought it cannot be so complicated to find God. Before, I had many, "I will die on the cross," moments in theological fact, until later I came to see that the fact was actually fiction. I had been told these facts so much over time that it had become a real "fact" of faith in my head. My head was hurting trying to find the answers to life's simple problems. But it was far from simple or so it seemed.

Simplicity is defined in *The American Heritage Dictionary* (1976) as,

"The state or quality of being simple; absence of complexity, intricacy, or artificiality."

Complexity and artificiality are not what usually comes to mind when one is trying to find an answer to a real problem one is facing. I was there and still am. God's future plans for me could not be that complex if he is trying to communicate those plans to me in real time. I remember reading a book by Dick Eastman, director of Every Home for Christ, and how he learned about the simplicity of God's guidance in his first missionary trip to British Honduras, or as it is called now, Belize. He wrote,

As we walked from house to house in the shimmering heat of Belize City, the capital, we noticed people's hunger for the printed page. Not one person rejected the literature. Often those who were home wanted to hear more. We were amazed when more than 450 people in just five weeks invited us into their homes and prayed to receive Christ as Savior.

Late one night in the sweltering heat, I lay awake thinking about the simplicity of communicating the Gospel house to house and unusual receptivity of the people. Why wasn't there a worldwide initiative to do just what we were doing? It seemed

so logical, especially after 450 people had prayed to receive Christ in just over a month. At that time as many as three million people globally were becoming literate every week. How relatively easy it would be to evangelize the vast majority of the world, I thought, if the global Church went systematically to where people lived, providing them a clearly printed message of salvation…..How simple it would be…[1]

He found "simple" in the sense that it is not complex, not in the sense that it is juvenile or childish. I too longed for the simple, the definitive, the understandable, and the truth. In a quote by Leo Babauta, **"Simplicity boils down to two steps: Identify the essential. Eliminate the rest."** [2]And that is what I was endeavoring to do.

---

[1] Eastman, D. (2012). *Look What God is Doing*. Colorado Springs, Colorado: Every Home for Christ, p. 69.

[2] Babuata, L. *Quote on Simplicity*. Leobabuata.com.

However, during the hippie era of the 60's and 70's, I was confused, and I argued about everything and with everyone, making the simple debatable, and controversial. One time I was so arrogant in my truth of the moment, that I took on a Marine colonel in a debate on the divine truth of non-violence and the totally sinfulness of war. I was elated when people told me I "nailed" him in my discussion. Only later in life when I was caught in a civil war in an overseas country, I came to understand that there are not simply good guys and bad guys. Sometimes, there are bad guys, good guys, and really bad guys. I may have been wrong.

So, as I got older, I wanted to find the "bottom line" on Christian thought and social norms and then do my best to live in those principles that Christ gave as this basis of living. I have come to see Christianity in a much more basic "this is what you need to believe." Not that I have grown more of an intellect than my fellow man and now understand it all, in fact, I understand less. I know for sure only what I have seen, heard, and experienced, and outside of that, most of the rest of my theological leaning is supposition. It is pretty simple for me.

I know God, and I know man, and I am beginning to know me. I have had my "Moses on the mountain" (Exodus 19) experience, and I have had my Elijah moment in the "dark night of the soul" (I Kings 18) event. I have voiced my opinions as Peter (John 13) and John (Luke 9) in the height of arrogance and pride and I have had to repent over and over again. I have had the "Thomas" (John 20) doubt and I have also seen the healing of the "man crippled from birth" (Acts 3). I have been there, and I was that man. I have been on the mountain and I have been in the valley. I have looked for answers and found only one, or so I thought, but in actuality I have found that there are two answers, and this is my basis for this book.

Since working as a counselor, pastor, teacher, and missionary, I have tended to deal with two basic tenets of life that appear in most everyone's personal and  spiritual adjustment in my counseling of these clients. The first one deals with a person's relationship with God and the other is the person's relationship with others, with each tenet giving equally to the maturity and health of one's relationship with oneself. As I studied, I have found from academic research and personal anecdotal interaction that you cannot separate the relationships that exist from God to man and from man to man. They are so interconnected that if you try to address only the God given relationship and ignore the social development with man, you will become maladjusted and various vices will appear and dysfunction will develop. Communion with God and community with mankind are inseparable, and they are also inseparable from knowing yourself. How we deal with each other appears to be so linked with our righteousness with God that you must do both to maintain order in one's life. Jesus quotes from the Old Testament when he tells us the greatest commandment as he teaches his disciples:

"You shall love the Lord your God with all your heart, with all your soul, and with all your mind. This is the first and great commandment.

And then Jesus adds a little more…

And the second is like it: 'You shall love your neighbor as yourself."
(Matthew 22:37-39).

Man, and God are so interlinked that you must fulfill both commands to be holistically complete. The apostle John continues in this same vein of thought as he outlines the command in even greater detail,

"And this commandment we have from Him: that he who loves God must love his brother also."
(John 4:21.)

Since I lived in the Middle East for many years and have observed the various customs and mores practiced there, I have come to realize that we in the West separate spiritual development and social customs into separate categories of behavior, both religiously and psychologically. There is the spiritual man, psychological man, and the social man. We act as individuals that live in one body but entertain two personalities: one for God and one for man. It causes conflict within oneself and with others, as well as with God. Then personality disorders begin to appear that causes us pain, hurt, and a disarray in our feelings and functioning. We can see this from the Bible as well, for those that have tried to act this way have failed, as they tried to live in two worlds, with each causing internal strife in the person so inclined.

There are rules however, that govern both areas of our lives and are connected even from the beginning of time. Let us start with what God's rules are, as outlined in the Bible in Exodus 20, as we highlight the "Ten Commandments" given of old. These commandments are a set of rules given in the Old Testament to govern the relationship of God to man and from man to man. It is interesting that the first commandment to top the list is the one that says,

"You shall have no other gods before Me."
(Exodus 20:3 NKJV).

This commandment is first and supersedes all the others and is the basis for the observance of any additional rules that govern our behavior. If we do not believe God is, and that this particular God interacts in the affairs of man, then all the remainder of the commandments have no meaning or justification for application. There can be no other Gods, no other extreme longings, no other acknowledgement of power, except that of God; the one God as seen in the Bible. There can be no true self without the self that is rooted in the superiority and reverence of God almighty. God cannot bless that which is not his and if we are not God's, except through the grace of God, we cannot be blessed. In this first command we must have nothing else that comes between us and God, not ourselves, not others, nor anything that removes God from his place of prominence and worship.

However, the Bible continues with other commandments relating to our relationship with God;

 # 2: "You shall not make for yourself a carved image – any likeness of anything that is in heaven above, or that is in the earth beneath, or that is in the water under the earth; you shall not bow down to them or serve them...."

As one writer comments,

"In the Bible, the sin of idolatry is not just a matter of bowing down to statues. Idol worship is treating the work of your hands as if it were divine, worshipping *yourself* as the highest source of value and creativity. When the second commandment reads, "You shall not make yourself a graven image," one commentator takes that to mean not "You shall not make an idol for yourself," but "You shall not make an idol of yourself." Do not make yourself into an object of worship by believing that you have enough power to control the world in which you live and the other people who live in it." [3]

Otto Baab in, *"The Theology of the Old Testament"* (1949) writes,

---

[3] Kushner, H. (1986). *When All You've Ever Wanted Isn't Enough.* New York, New York: Summit Books, p. 53.

"When an idol is worshipped, man is worshipping himself, his desires, his purpose and his will....As a consequence of this type of idolatry man was outrageously guilty of giving himself the status of God and exalting his own will as of supreme worth." [4]

We engage in self-talk about our God likeness, and tell ourselves how good we are intrinsically, when all the while knowing we are not. "Self-talk" about how wonderful you are doesn't work if the next day the real you, and the situation entertained, remains the same."[5] We are not gods, only human, and we do not have the answers outside of a relationship with God, and so the commandments continue,

---

[4] Baab, O. (1949). *The Theology of the Old Testament.* New York, New York: Abingdon/Cokesbury.

[5] Vitz, P. (1977). *Psychology as Religion, The Cult of Self-Worship.* Grand Rapids, Michigan: William B. Eerdmans Publishing Company, p. 131.

3: "You shall not take the name of your God in vain…" (Exodus 20:7).

4: "Remember the Sabbath to keep it holy…" (Exodus 20:8).

They each deal with our interdependence upon God. But then the nature and character of the commandments takes a change in thought and direction and for the next six commandments, they address how we interact, man to man.

5: Honor your father and your mother, that your days may be long upon the land which the Lord your God is giving you. # 6: You shall not murder. # 7: You shall not commit adultery. # 8: You shall not steal. # 9: You shall not bear false witness against your neighbor. # 10: You shall not covet your neighbor's house; you shall not covet your neighbor's wife, nor his male servant, nor his female servant, nor his ox, nor his donkey, nor anything that is your neighbor's."
(Exodus 20:12-17).

God and man are internally and externally joined together in one set of commandments. We are not two individuals in one body, but we are one as God is one in a similar trinitarian nature with a needed relationship with God, others, and ourselves and totally interconnected in purpose and activity. We are whole, complete and anything outside of this totality will result in an inability to function normally. As said, "One human being is no human being," and "One person without God is nobody."

One thing that I would like for you to notice, that you may have missed, and that is; the commandments in the Old Testament starts with God first; the Communion with God, and then it leads into the Community of Man. Then again, in the New Testament, when Jesus is asked about the greatest command; it starts again with God first and it ends with Man. Later, when John is renewed with a fresh vision of God in the book of Revelation; it starts with God and ends with man. When Moses is confronted with himself as he turns aside to see the voice from the burning bush in the desert; we find that it starts with God and it ends with man. The same it is with Elijah; it starts with God and ends with man. There can be nothing outside of Jesus that leads one to have Community with Man. It is not a social club, it is not a committee, it is not a business with its shareholders, it is not a school with its pupils, but real community can only be accomplished when one is right with God. Then and only then is one is right with man. We then can be complete, healed, whole, well, sane, and with a balanced life, or as some say, "we will have it together."

"Community means community through Jesus Christ and in Jesus Christ. No Christian community is more or less than this. Whether it is a brief encounter or the daily fellowship of years, Christian community is only this. We belong to one another only through and in Jesus Christ," [6] as

---

[6] Bonhoeffer, D. (1954). *Life Together*. New York, New York: HarperCollins Publishers, p. 21.

stated by Dietrich Bonhoeffer in his book, *"Life Together"* (1954).

So, what is Communion with God? It is a sharing of all one's self and an interaction with your creator that links your heart to His. It is listening, not just to your heart but to the Word of God that is speaking through his scriptures. We know and experience God.

The Bible proclaims in Ephesians 2:14 that,

"For He Himself is our peace, who has made both one, and has broken down the middle wall of separation."

Therefore, starting with this peace, we move into God's presence with assurance that we are God's workmanship, created in Christ for good works, (Eph. 2:10). We are made by him, loved by him, redeemed by him, and joined with him to do all that he created us to do. Christ no longer calls us servants, he calls us friends and, in the plural, for we cannot stand alone but only in the Community of Man. Outside of Christ we can do nothing and outside of knowing others who call Jesus, Lord, we can know nothing.

Which leads us to the Community of Man. We are brothers and sisters in the Lord because we have the same Father. We are not in a religious fellowship, but we are in a family that provides the community and comfort of knowing that there in the presence of God and man, we can succeed in life. The Bible tells us to confess our faults one to another, or as some translations say, confess our sins to one another. You thought sin was only between you and God, but it is not. It is a double faceted approach to God. In Matthew 6 Jesus teaches the disciples how to pray,

Our father in heaven,

Hallowed be Your name.

Your kingdom come.

Your will be done

On earth as it is in heaven.

Give us this day our daily bread.

And forgive us our debts,

As we forgive our debtors.

And do not lead us into temptation,

But deliver us from the evil one.

For yours is the kingdom and the

Power and the glory forever, Amen.[7]

As you can see there is not a personal pronoun anywhere in the prayer for it is an "us" prayer, only to be prayed when you are in Communion with God and in Community with Man. This idea of "Jesus as your personal savior" may not be a complete Biblical affirmation. We as Westerners make Christ like an idol of our own thinking. As we understood earlier, this sort of thinking is against the second commandment of the first ten commandments given. The Bible says, Christ came to save sinners, of whom I am chief, (I Tim. 1:15), and notice again it is in the

---

[7] *The Holy Bible, New King James Version* (1982). Nashville, TN.: Thomas Nelson Publishers.

idea of us, sinners in the collective, not just me. I have heard preachers say, "If I was the only person on earth, Jesus would have died just for me." Which of course puts the emphasis on me, the individual. They say, "I am that important." For real? Christ came into the world to save the world, and we just happen to be in that group of people we call the world. Community is not an idea or a way of life, it is a fulfillment of what Christ wants in our lives. It is not a fellowship of believers, no, it is obeying of what God has commanded and admonished us to pray for. It is a community of believers in Christ. We cannot stand alone, without Christ or without our brother. This is a package deal. It is Communion with God and Community with Man.

In light of this application, we are now going to examine some of the personalities of the Bible and see how they came to understand the nature of God and their relationships with God and man. Starting with God and proceeding to the fellowship with man and our relationship to both God and man, we will move to a deeper understanding of the "Kingdom of God." We will also examine how they lived in a community of people in a way that expressed positive behavioral changes in them and in those with whom they interacted. So, come now, and let us follow some of the more colorful characters of the Bible and watch their transformation from god-less to godly, from selfish to self-less, from dysfunction to normalcy, with each resulting in a right relationship with both God and man. Let us see how they are transformed into having a faith not born out of answers to their questions but born out of a relationship that refuses to even ask the question. Communion with God is going to be developed by God himself at His invitation, then Community with Man will be developed by us at our initiative.

CHAPTER ONE

Moses, the Lawgiver: From Hostility to Humility

We will begin our story of Moses in the book of Numbers when Moses is older, and then we will return and back track, fill in the blanks, and come to understand the most important parts missing in the story. In Numbers 12:1-9, there is the story of Moses and his interaction with Aaron his brother and Miriam his sister, who as a trio of prophets have come face to face with God:

Then Miriam and Aaron spoke against Moses because of the Ethiopian woman whom he had married; for he had married an Ethiopian woman. So they said, "Has the Lord indeed spoken only through Moses? Has he not spoken through us

also?" And the Lord heard it. (Now the man Moses was very humble, more than all men who were on the face of the earth.) Suddenly the Lord said to Moses, Aaron, and Miriam, "Come out, you three, to the tabernacle of meeting!" So the three came out. Then the Lord came down in the pillar of cloud and stood in the door of the tabernacle, and called Aaron and Miriam. And they both went forward. Then he said,

"Hear now My words:
If there is a prophet among you
I, the Lord, make Myself known to him in a vision
I speak to him in a dream.
Not so with My servant Moses,
He is faithful in all My house.
I speak with him face to face,
Even plainly, and not in dark sayings;
And he sees the form of the Lord.
Why were you then not afraid
To speak against My servant Moses?"

So the anger of the Lord was aroused against them, and He departed.
(Numbers 12:1-9 NKJV)

In these verses we find the family in dispute over Moses' new wife, an Ethiopian or Kushite, that remains unnamed. Zipporah, his first wife, has died and Moses has married a new wife, a Kushite, an Ethiopian of the Sudan. The Kushite kingdom had ruled Sudan during the time of the Exodus and the many pyramids of the Sudan still seen today attest to the remarkable magnitude of this vast kingdom. Later between 744-656 BC, the new Kingdom of Cush or Kush, would arise again as the "Black Pharaohs" or the 25th Dynasty of Egypt and would reign over, not just the Sudan, but all of Egypt. The Kushites were not seen in the worldview which later the black races would come to be associated with, that is, slavery. The Kushites were anything except slaves. Moses' Kushite wife was unnamed in the Bible and we do not know much about her, except as seen in the various references we see here. We do know that she was probably darker than the Jewish people of the Exodus, and this would cast doubt and suspicion as to the nature of Moses' marriage when viewed by Moses' brother and sister. But she was not by any means of lower status, class wise, except as seen by Aaron and Miriam. Aaron, Moses's brother, and Miriam, his sister, were proud of their status as prophets and as ethnic "Hebrews" and they used this example from Moses' marriage as a ploy to call into question his status as prophet over them.

They asked Moses about God's favor and questioned the interaction that Moses had as a prophet with God. They were jealous and envious of the position that Moses held, along with his wife.

"Has He not spoken through us also?" (Numbers 12:2) Aaron and Miriam asked as they paraded their arrogance and vanity as prophets.

However, in contrast to their arrogance, Moses, the Bible says, was just the opposite,

Now the man Moses was very humble, more than all men who were on the face of the earth. (Numbers 12:3).

The Bible wants us to know "off the record," (The quote originally is in parenthesis), of how God saw Moses. However, we want to know more. We want to know and understand how he got to that place of humility and favor. How did Moses get to this pedestal of humility and meekness that was unequal in all mankind for which the Bible only alludes to? How did Moses grow into a mature, well-adjusted individual, satisfied and content with who he was and how he lived? How was he to find favor with God and man?

Moses' life story begins with the story of his genealogy, telling us in Exodus 2 that he was born to Amram to Jochebed, his wife, in Egypt, during a time of social upheaval. This was the Amarna Age (1500 B.C.) the name taken from the Pharaoh, Akhnaton, and a time when the ruling powers had achieved a balance of power in the Middle East. It was a time of great wealth and grandeur and into this era, Moses grew.

However, since the time of Joseph and the immigration of Joseph's immediate Hebrew family to Egypt over 400 years prior, the people of Israel in Egypt had grown into a population of millions. This vast number were now the slaves to the Egyptians and racial discord became evident. The Israelites or Hebrew people had grown into disfavor with the Pharaoh and the Pharaoh had ordered that all baby boys born to the "Hebrew" women be thrown into the Nile river and be killed or sacrificed. The Egyptians worshiped the Nile River as a God and this infanticide could be seen as child sacrifice to this God of the Nile. Furthermore, the Egyptians feared that the Hebrew population was of such magnitude that they could rise in rebellion and overthrow their Egyptian leaders and slave masters, therefore the balance of power must be maintained.

Moses, however, was saved from this infanticide when his mother designed a basket of reeds that would float on the Nile, which through divine providence, would eventually lead Moses to safety. In the divine plan of God, Moses was found floating on the river by Pharaoh's daughter and he was brought into Pharaoh's house, the ruler of all of Egypt, and his life was spared.

He was given the name Moses, or Mosheh in Hebrew, which could mean, "one drawn, (Hebrew-Mashah) from the water," or it could be interpreted as well as a "God who came from the Nile or born from the Nile." Moses with the "ses" suffix is similar to the use of the same suffix in the name, Rameses, a name for a line of Pharaohs most people are familiar with. This name would give Moses a godly distinction to himself and would cause even a deeper divide in Moses' thinking since he knew he was not a God. Moses is also pronounced Mw-se, which also has the connotation in the language of the Egyptians of royalty and divinity. He was royal, but he was not divine.

He was raised as a member of Pharaoh's household but was nursed and cared for by Moses' own mother, Jochebed, in a scheme that belittles a mystery movie. He lived for 40 years under the auspices of the Pharaoh's leadership and according to tradition, he became the military envoy that led Egypt's army into many successful battles. In Acts 7:22, Luke mentions Moses' educational credentials in the address by Stephen to the Sanhedrin,

"And Moses was learned in all the wisdom of the Egyptians, and was mighty in words and deeds."

In this address by Stephen he asserted that Moses was not only instructed in the science and learning of the Egyptians, but he also was endowed with leadership skills and a certain quality of distinction. He would have been educated in the courts of the Pharaohs that provided their pupils teaching and training from all the city- states of Egypt that extended as far north as the Euphrates River. [8] He was both a "Hebrew" and an "Egyptian" and yet he was out of place in both cultures, which soon became evident as the conflict emerged in his own personality. He did not know how to deal with the two nationalities that battled internally. He is the first child in the Bible that is recorded to have been "abandoned." He was the ultimate foster child so to speak. He had an Egyptian name and a Jewish mother. He had Jewish roots, but with a Pharaoh's prestige. He was troubled and in pain as both sides fought for dominance in his own psychic and soul, with Moses not knowing which way to turn. It was

---

[8] Tenney, M. (1963). *The Zondervan Pictorial Bible Dictionary*. Grand Rapids, Michigan: Zondervan Publishing House, p. 557.

out of this pain that he made a decision that would affect his life from then on and cause him to have to flee Egypt and go into exile. In his life as a biracial person of multi-ethnicity, each ethnic group in Egypt distrusted his intentions and called into question his each and every move.

Egyptian Hieroglyph of Slaves Making Bricks

Therefore, in Exodus, Chapter Two, we read where Moses' personality conflict pushes him into the beginnings of a psychological and spiritual dilemma. He sees a Hebrew slave being beaten by an Egyptian slave master and Moses in his anger and racial identification proceeds to kill the Egyptian in order to protect his Hebrew brethren. He hides the Egyptian in fear and buries him in the sand and the fear cycle of depression and mental anguish begins to burden his heart and soul. It is a normal psychological phenomenon as seen in the pain to depression diagnosis, with Moses at just the beginning of the cycle.

In the book, *Lonely, Sad, and Angry,* (1995) by Ingersoll and Goldstein, they relate how the lineation from lonely to depression can manifest itself even from early childhood. Can we say for certain that this had happened in Moses? In retrospect, we do not know for sure, but we do know from scripture that when Moses killed the slave master, he was alone in the desert, or so he thought, and he was sad, and he was angry. Ingersoll and Goldstein relate that if these feelings of loneliness and sadness are prolonged over time and overwhelm the individual, then depression must be considered, and for Moses this dilemma had been boiling for forty years. He first manifested the classic fight in the "fight and flight" syndrome in his beating of the slave master as he fought to save his Hebrew "brother," but then he took the second half in flight, when he fled to Midian in exile.

Let me give you a simple illustration to explain Moses and how this loneliness, sadness, fear, anger, and depression cycle begins. Let us pretend you are a carpenter and are building a house, something you have done for years. As Moses, you are in your forties, assured and confident in your work. You have swung a hammer for years without accident as you have built houses from the initial framework to the finished product, but today it is going to be different. As you begin this day, with your hammer in hand, you miss the nail on your first swing and hit your thumb. Immediately and without thought, pain pours through your thumb, and with a shaking of the hand and an illicit word in your mouth, you acknowledge the hurt and you get angry at yourself for being so careless. It is automatic without any thinking on your part. Then this pain and hurt takes you to the next step on your road to anger.

You begin again, and once more, without knowing why, you hit your finger, and in pain and anger you cry out one more time. You are disgusted with yourself and you question your abilities, but you go on. You are a good carpenter and you know how to do this. However, the third time you try to hit the nail, you do the same thing, striking your finger with an even harder blow. But this time the pain and hurt is more than just a physical pain, it becomes a fear. A fear that if you try to hammer the nail again, you know it will have the same dire results. You fear you are not really a good carpenter, and you begin to be anxious and question your abilities as a worker. You wonder if you are getting too old for the job. You question if something is physically wrong with you. You may blame it on the argument you had with your spouse before you left for work this morning, and you are in this cycle of pain – anger – sadness - fear and if you are not careful, it will lead you into depression. It will be at that place where you question who you are, not just as a worker, but as an individual. You will say to yourself, "What will I do if I cannot be a carpenter anymore, and who will pay the bills, and how will my kids be taken care of? I have a car note and a mortgage and how will that get paid?" The list goes on in your head. You can find yourself clinically depressed with psychological and spiritual disabilities, all beginning with a sequence of unfavorable results from an action that you sought to undertake.

I know it is a simplistic illustration, but in my clinical work as a counselor, when someone comes to the clinic and they say they are depressed, I always ask about pain and anger. I want to know what they are fearful of and who are they bitter at and angry with. Are they mad at someone or maybe they are mad at God? It appears that pain, hurt, anger, fear, and depression are always the best of friends. If I find someone depressed, I have found a person who is angry at something.

And that is where we find Moses. Follow me as I follow Moses over the next stages of his life, and we will explore how he started as an angry, fearful man and how he ended as the humblest man of his time as written in the Old Testament scriptures in Numbers 12.

We had left Moses in Exodus 2, where he had just killed an Egyptian who was beating a Hebrew slave. Moses in his anger and in his empathy with the burdens that his Hebrew brethren were feeling, came to the decision to kill the slave master, hide his body in the Sahara sand, and then return again to his life as Pharaoh's son. However, his murder of the slave master did not go unnoticed, for the very next day when he tried to intervene in a quarrel between two Hebrew slaves, they remarked,

"Who made you a prince and a judge over us? Do you intend to kill me as you killed the Egyptian?"
(Exodus 2:14).

Both sides in this racial divide saw Moses as the enemy. He was caught between his Hebrew ethnicity and his Egyptian upbringing and he had the ultimate foster child breakdown. He felt torn between two worlds, two families, and two identities. He decided to run away from Egypt, away from the problem, and therefore he ran away from who he was as well. He went into exile into the land of Midian and here again he is faced with trouble and a moral dilemma.

In his new country of immigration, he comes upon a well that was used by various families, and there at the well, two clans are vying for power for the use of this precious commodity of water for their sheep herds. Moses comes upon the violent exchange of the men shepherds and the other shepherds who are women, and Moses proceeds to take the side of the ladies. He intervenes and takes on the men trying to usurp the local daughters of Jethro and their use of the well. Moses in his anger, however a productive anger at this time, again enters into the conflict by driving the men away and is successful in saving the day for the daughters of Jethro. Moses has a strict sense of justice and of right and wrong, but here it is displayed in a constructive use of his anger. Back in Egypt he tried once before to intervene by using his power and anger and it went sour, but this time Moses was the hero of the day as he helped some helpless daughters of Midian to water their sheep. He drove away the antagonists and saved the day for the young maidens in need. (Exodus 2). And he was rewarded for his behavior. Anger could not be that bad, he thought. He was now 40 years of age, in a new country, with new friends, but he was also at a turning point in his life.

He is invited to stay in Midian in present day Saudi Arabia. (Some say the Midianites were the "Shasu" people as referenced by two inscriptions found in Egypt that talk of the "Shasu of yhwh." They are the oldest know references to Yahweh outside of the Bible.) [9] We do know from the Bible that the Midianites were in fact distant cousins of Moses through Keturah, the wife of Abraham (Genesis 25:1-6).

Moses took one of Jethro's (also called Reuel) daughters, Zipporah, to be his wife and then proceeded to shepherd the sheep of his new father-in-law, Jethro, for the next 40 years. He remained in serfdom under Jethro and continued under his care and support. Over the years, Zipporah bore him children, but yet through all of this he remained in this stage of development that kept him in this depressive mood that manifested itself in a lack of purpose. He never got his own flock of sheep, his own reason for being, and he never became more than just an "on call" shepherd tending his father-in-law's sheep. Later, when naming his first son, Gershom,

---

[9] Friedman, R. (2017). *The Exodus*. New York, New York: Harper One Publishers, p. 122.

Moses chose that particular name for he felt alone and out of place. As the Bible tells us in Exodus 2:22,

And she bore him a son. He called his name Gershom, for he said. "I have been a stranger in a foreign land.
(Exodus 2:22)

Moses was feeling like an alien, a foreigner, and an outcast for he had been just that for the last forty years. He was still angry and now at eighty years of age he was neither a Hebrew, an Egyptian, or a Midianite. He was like a confused child, living in the past, and afraid of the future.

Piaget, the famous developmental psychologist, says there are three stages of human development and we have followed Moses as he transitions between the three. First, he is in the "childhood" phase where one listens to authority unquestionably and follows whoever is in authority. Then one moves into the "adolescent" phase where we begin to question everything, and we do our own thing. This was the phase Moses was in when he killed the slave master in the desert 40 years ago, and now we are going to see Moses begin his long transition into "adulthood," the third stage of development. Now, starting at age 80 and moving onward until he is 120 years of age, we will watch him develop and mature in himself and in his faith. This is the phase where he will ask others for help and make decisions with the advice of God and of man. He will move from doing what he can do, to what he should do, and there is where maturity lies. However, this is not where Moses is at this point, but he does take the first step, or so it appears. However, in reality, it was God who took the first step and Moses reluctantly follows. These next few years of experiencing life on the road, leading the Exodus, and caring for God's people does not make Moses immediately humble as stated by the Bible in Numbers 12, but as you see, this is the time when he begins to see, not how he sees himself, nor how others see him, but how God sees him.

We will now turn back to the Bible seeking answers to Moses' life and his maturity in walking with God. Presently, he is still in the adolescent stage of development and he is still governed by the fear he is experiencing and feeling. But in Exodus 3, God reveals himself to Moses, starting with the burning bush experience that Moses turns aside to see in the desert. It is a burning bush that never extinguished and while Moses turned aside to investigate the phenomena, he has an encounter with God, and the healing process begins. This God is not the God of nature as worshipped by the Egyptians, this God is a God known by his history and his words to his people. He is above nature, and this God, Jehovah, calls him out and tells him,

"I am the God of your father – the God of Abraham, the God of Isaac, and the God of Jacob."
(Exodus 3:6).

God reveals who he was in the past and now he also tells Moses that he exists eternally in the present as well as the future by revealing to Moses his name: I AM WHO I AM. Here is God speaking to the common man, eternal truths, not to kings and priests, but to a shepherd tending sheep on a mountain. He is God Jehovah, the YHWH or Yahweh, the creator God.

Moses and the Burning Bush

Moses responds by hiding his face, for he was afraid to look upon God. But it was in that first face to face meeting with God that God gave Moses his ethnic identity as God says, **"I am the God of your father,"** and he lists the early heroes of the Hebrew faith. Moses was no longer a foster child, for he now understood that he was from a long line of patriarchs and that these men of renown were his ancestors and family.

In *Everyman's Talmud,* (Cohen, 1887), the author relates that one must,

"Reflect upon three things and you will not come under the power of sin; know whence you came, and whither you are going, and before Whom you will in the future have to give account and reckoning."

(p. 217).

Moses was there in this time of reflection and interaction for he was face to face with God as God spoke to Moses for the first time out of the burning bush. God was showing Moses where he came from, who he was, and who he was going to be.

None the less, Moses is still afraid and in verse 11 of Exodus 3, Moses asks out of his inferiority,

"Who am I that I should go to Pharaoh?"

He is paralyzed in his fear, running on the lonely-anger to depression wheel that keeps him from following God and the destiny that God has set before him.

Moses still had his inferior complex, was fearful, and is still in the adolescent stage of personality and spiritual development. He questions God, makes excuses, talks of his inadequacies, says he cannot communicate well since he is "slow of tongue."

Many believe he had a stutter or a lisp, or some sort of speech defect. However, when one looks at this idiom in the only other place where it is mentioned in the Bible, in Ezekial3:6, where it alludes to those "deep in lip and heavy in tongue," it signifies a lack of knowing the foreign language of the people to which one is going. Moses as well may be saying that he has been away from the Hebrew people and the Egyptians, and he does not speak the language well. Again, this would coincide with his lack of confidence and his feelings of alienation, leaving Moses once again the foster child of prophets, not knowing where he stands in the eyes of the people in Egypt, both Hebrew and Egyptian. He believes no one will accept him or his calling. He tells God to please send someone else. Humble yet, not quite, but afraid, yes. Angry? Yes. Uncertain? Yes. Lost? Yes.

In the book by Meier, Minirth, and Wichern, *"Introduction to Psychology and Counseling, Christian Perspectives and Applications"* (1982),[10] five symptoms are listed that designate a diagnosis of depression: sad affect, painful thinking, physical symptoms, anxiety, and delusional thinking. Moses had experienced all of these by this time in his life with the end result being disassociated and at times in despair. On page 263 in the same book, Meier lists the levels of anxiety on a grading scale of 1-100 that can

---

[10] Meier, P., Minirth, F., Wichern, F. (1982). *Introduction to Psychology and Counseling.* Grand Rapids, Michigan: Baker Book House.

trigger depression and despair into one's life. In a grading scale, the following events of Moses' life can be examined and applied to that same scale:

- **Death of a spouse - 100**
- **Death of close family member – 63**
- **Change to a different line of work – 36**
- **Change in responsibilities at work – 29**
- **Change in living conditions – 25**
- **Revision of personal habits – 24**
- **Change in residence – 20**
- **Change in eating habits – 15**

We look at these in jest in some ways, but Moses was under such a strain as the "Let my people go," leader that something had to change for the better. He was experiencing all of these anecdotal factors, and the numbers added up. Something had to change, and something **did** change that affected Moses forever and for the better. He will be examining the revelation of this change agent in the years to come, but it started at the very beginning of his ministry and leadership.

It is just a small word in the middle of a verse that does not seem to be a major life changer, but it was. In Exodus 4:10 in a verse that you may overlook, we find that Moses makes a statement that changes his entire perspective on his work, himself, and his life. He has heard God say,

"I am the God of your fathers – the God of Abraham, the God of Isaac, and the God of Jacob." (Exodus 3:6).

But was God, the God of Moses? God was the God of his ancestors, but now Moses sees and understands that God is the God of Moses too. Moses first acknowledges God as his Lord when he says,

Then Moses said to the Lord, "O MY (my emphasis) LORD, I am not eloquent, neither before nor since You have spoken to Your servant;

but I am slow in speech and slow in tongue. (Exodus 4:10).

This is the first time Moses has called God his personal Lord. It seems insignificant, but it is the start of Moses' transformation into a leader, this man of humility, the same Moses that would one day stand with Christ on the Mount of Transfiguration, this patriarch of both Christians and Jews. This was the beginning of a new Moses. However, Moses still argues with God over his lack of abilities, his lack of confidence, his inability to speak eloquently, and his lack of knowledge. There is a lot of the old Moses in this new Moses, but God continues in his instruction, guidance, and his maturing of Moses.

It seems odd that in two chapters later, in Exodus 6, the Bible shares an episode that appears to be seemingly out of place. It is here once again that God is still reassuring Moses of who Moses is and who He as God is. In Exodus 6:2, God speaks again, and he says,

"I am the Lord. I appeared to Abraham, to Isaac, and to Jacob, as God Almighty, but by My name Lord I was not known to them.... I am the Lord; I will bring you out from under the burdens of the Egyptians, I will rescue you from their bondage, I will redeem you with an outstretched arm and with great judgement."
(Exodus 6:2-6).

God was doing a new thing, with a new name as Lord, the Lord; a Lord to be known by instruction or observation,[11] and he was going to do this teaching under the auspices of Moses. Moses is going to organize a people into a nation, a theocracy. (Theocracy comes from two Greek words, theos and kratos, meaning a rule by God himself.)

---

[11] Zodhiades, S. (1990). *The Hebrew- Greek Key Study Bible*. Chattanooga, TN.: AMG Publishers.

Again, right in the middle of Exodus 6, God continues to uplift Moses with a genealogical survey of Moses' family and God says,

"These are the same Aaron and Moses to whom the Lord said…" and then ends the chapter with, "These are the same Moses and Aaron."
(Exodus 6:14-27).

(Note that now the writer of Exodus lists Moses first over his older brother, Aaron, of three years.) Yes, this is the Moses that you all know, it is him.

Notwithstanding, God is not through with Moses. He takes him through the ten plagues that decimate Egypt and its' gods. God answers Moses' prayers before and after each plague and Moses watches as Pharaoh and his army, the very one that he has commanded in his youth, come to an end in the Red Sea. However, Moses is still a man in conflict as he battles his personal and spiritual shortcomings. He is still an angry man. He gets angry at the Hebrew nation, struggling in its infancy. He remains an angry man, and he is still not the "humblest of men that have ever lived."

In Exodus 32 when Moses is coming down from Mt. Sinai with the two tablets of commandments in his hand, he sees the people dancing and the golden calf

set in the midst of the camp, and in his hot anger he casts the tablets down breaking them into pieces. In the same chapter Aaron says,

"Do not let the anger of my lord become hot."
(Exodus 32:22).

People knew Moses, not for his humility, but for his anger. Even thousands of years later when you see

Moses drawn by various artists and sculptors, he is drawn or pictured as a man with an angry disposition. In fact, you will see in paintings from the Renaissance that they portray Moses as having horns, but this is not representative of his anger, but was a Latin mistranslation that said that Moses upon his return from Mount Sinai had "horns emanating from his head," when in actuality in later translations, they corrected it and spoke of "rays of light" protruding from his face.[12] At least Moses was honestly misrepresented at the time of the Middle Ages and later corrected.

However, in Numbers 20:11, as the Children of Israel enter the Wilderness of Zin, and they find themselves without water again, and they begin to complain to Moses and Aaron. God instructs Moses to speak to the rock that is before him and water

---

[12] Kidder, D., Oppenheim, N. (2006). *The Intellectual Devotional.* New York, New York: Rodale, p. 56.

would come flowing out, but Moses in his anger struck the rock with his staff, disobeying God.

And Moses and Aaron gathered the assembly together before the rock; and he said to them, "Hear now, you rebels! Must we bring water for you out of this rock?" Then Moses lifted his hand and struck the rock twice with his rod; and water came out abundantly, and the congregation and their animals drank. Then the Lord spoke to Moses and Aaron, "Because you did not believe Me, to hallow Me in the eyes of the children of Israel, therefore you shall not bring the assembly into the land which I have given them"
(Exodus 20:10-12).

Later Moses was punished for this angry misbehavior, and Moses because of this misdeed, would never be allowed to go into the promised land. He would die and be buried on the wrong side of the Jordon River at Mount Nebo, paying the ultimate price for his anger and its display.

It appears if looking at Moses through the eyes of Piaget, we would have to say that Moses is still in the adolescent state of personal and spiritual development. He is growing into maturity and adulthood, but it is not an easy task. None the less, He begins to see that he cannot do it on his on and even with God's leadership and help he still needs those around him to provide him support. He must have a relationship with God and a relationship with man.

For example, when he fights against Amalek in Exodus 17 Moses tells Joshua,

"Choose us some men and go out and fight with Amalek. Tomorrow I will stand on top of the hill with the rod of God in my hand. So Joshua did as Moses said to him and fought with Amalek. And Moses, Aaron, and Hur went up to the top of the hill. And so it was, when Moses held up his hand, that Israel prevailed; and when he let down his hand, Amalek prevailed. But Moses' hand became heavy; so they took a stone and put it under him,

and he sat on it. And Aaron and Hur supported his hands, one on one side, and the other on the other side; and his hands were steady until the going down of the sun. So Joshua defeated Amalek and his people with the edge of the sword.
(Exodus 17:8b-13).

Moses is finally understanding that instead of anger and conflict, cooperation and good leadership will go much further. He finds that seeking others to help will only strengthen their ability to get to their goal of entering the promised land.

Then in the very next chapter, Exodus 18, Moses in his exhausted state receives the advice of his father-in-law on the ruling and governing of the people of Israel. Moses at first thought that I have to do all of this governing on my own, but through the advice of Jethro, he delegates the ruling of judicial matters into the hands of good men that surround him and he finds that they too can be used of God to handle the conflicts that arise within such a mass of people.

Moses heard Jethro's counsel and instruction and he takes that advice. He asks those around him in leadership how to govern correctly and he listens to their words.

And Moses heeded the voice of his father-in-law and did all that he had said. And Moses chose able men out of all Israel, and made them heads over the people; rulers of thousands, rulers of hundreds, rulers of fifties, and rulers of tens. So they judged the people at all times; the hard cases they brought to Moses, but they judged every small case themselves. (Exodus 18:24-26).

Moses is learning even in his old age, and he is growing into an adult, a humble adult.

If you would ask those around Moses now, humility still would not be his most noticeable personality trait. Anger? Still there. Inferior complex? Still there. Fear? Still there. He struggles with his own nature and at times he falls back into the cycle of his old ways. But he is still growing.

Moses is now the chosen one, the leader, the spiritual head of Israel, and the redeemer of his people with God, his God, directing his every step. But it does not stop here, for this is just the beginning. Moses is looking, listening, and learning. In Exodus 33:11 the Bible says,

"So the Lord spoke to Moses face to face, as a man speaks to his friend."

God did not speak to Moses as a prophet or as a spokesperson, but as a friend. And God did converse over and over with Moses as his friend. Moses spoke with God in the Tabernacle, on the 40 years journey to Canaan, on Mount Sinai; the Mountain of God, and finally on Mount Nebo; the burial place of Moses. At times Moses was so close to God and to his glorious presence that the literal glory of God would shine through the face of Moses so bright that his face had to be veiled.

Now it was so, when Moses came down from Mount Sinai (and the two tablets of the testimony

were in Moses' hand when he came down from the mountain), that Moses did not know that the skin of his face shone while he talked with Him. So when Aaron and all the children of Israel saw Moses, behold, the skin of his face shone, and they were afraid to come near him....And when Moses had finished speaking with them, he put a veil on his face. (Exodus 34:29-33).

Moses wanted to be with God and God enjoyed the intimacy with Moses as well. Moses again and again took the relationship to an ever-deepening level as in Exodus 33:18 when Moses asked to see God's glory:

And he said, "Please show me your glory." Then he said, "I will make all My goodness pass before you, and I will proclaim the name of the Lord before you. I will be gracious to whom I will be gracious, and I will have compassion on whom I will have compassion." But He said, "You cannot see My face; for no man shall see Me, and live,"

And the Lord said, "Here is the place by Me, and you shall stand on the rock. So it shall be, while My glory passes by, that I will put you in the cleft of the rock, and will cover you with My hand while I pass by. Then I will take away My hand, and you shall see My back; but My face shall not be seen." (Exodus 33:18-23).

Moses sees God, hears God, senses God, and knows God like no one before him. He is more than a friend. Moses does not look at how others see him or as he sees himself, Moses wants to know how God sees him. It does not matter about his position or self-esteem, or his social position, nor his man-made goals. All that matters is his relationship with God. In Deuteronomy 34, Moses is told by God that he will not be entering into the land of Canaan but would die and be buried on Mount Nebo.

Then the Lord said to him, "This is the land of which I swore to give Abraham, Isaac, and Jacob, and saying, 'I will give it to your descendants.' I

have caused you to see it with your eyes, but you shall not cross over there." (Deuteronomy 34:4).

Moses does not argue, nor does he bargain and barter for another chance. By now, Moses knows God and trusts Him. He had spent time with God, 40 days straight at times with only God and him, and he has listened to God speak as one does face to face with a friend.

"But since then there has not arisen in Israel a prophet like Moses, whom the Lord knew face to face, (Deuteronomy 34:10).

But there is more, for Moses also grew in his maturity with man as well. Remember our premise at the beginning of the chapter: communion with God and community with man. Well, Moses now has his immediate family, with a wife and children, along with his brother Aaron and his sister Miriam, actively working together with Moses as prophets of God. Moses also has a father-in-law and a legacy of famous ancestors, and he has a people, a nation, the Hebrew nation, that he can identify with. He has helpers and friends, with Joshua and Hur being by his side, along with others who take responsibility and help him to lead. He has communion with God, but he also has a community of people that see him, trust him, and trust his God. Lonely, sad, depressed, are no more as he enters into his 120-year birthday facing his last days on earth and his eventual demise. He is not afraid. He is not angry. He is at peace with both God and man. He loves God and he loves man.

We know from Psalm 90 that Moses prayed for his people and you begin to experience in his own words his compassion and attitude toward his God and the Nation of Israel. Psalms 90:13-17, "the prayer of Moses, a man of God," clearly shows a man whose heart pleads for those he has come to love:

Return, O Lord!
How long?
And have compassion on Your servants.
Oh, satisfy us early with Your mercy,

That we may rejoice and be glad all our days!

Make us glad according to the days in which You

have afflicted us,

The years in which we have seen evil.

Let Your work appear to Your servants,

And Your glory to their children.

And let the beauty of the Lord our God be upon us,

And establish the work of our hands for us;

Yes, establish the work of our hands.

He has entered adulthood at old age, and he begins to show the change in his words and in his character.

So, let us return to our original premise in our discussion of Moses at the beginning of this chapter, and see how he became the most "humblest" of men. (Numbers 12:3). We have seen through the scriptures that God said he knew Moses by name, that they talked face to face even as friends, and that Moses even viewed the glory and goodness of God. Moses matured in his personality both in faith and in his relationships with God and man, and he listened and learned, becoming a man that truly knew God like no other before or after. He started asking for help from those around him and he sought out good leadership that he recognized in others. He had become that which God ordained him to be. He was,

(Now the man Moses was very humble, more than all men who were on the face of the earth.")
Numbers 12:3.

Albeit, that he had peace with God, he also had joy and a love as well for his people around him. Remember communion with God and community with man, well in Exodus 33, Moses has both and gives a blessing, not a curse to his people. These are the same people of the Exodus who complained, who followed after other gods, rebelled, and were a "mess" to deal with. Moses though, seems to have forgotten the troubles he experienced for he gives his blessings and tells the populace that God,

Yes, He loves the people; All his saints are in his hand; They sit down at your feet; Everyone receives Your words. (Deuteronomy 33:3).

Then he begins to name the tribes one by one and extends platitudes to each name:

- Reuben: **Let Reuben live and not die, Nor let his men be few (vs. 6).**

- Judah: **Let his hands be sufficient for him, And may You be a help against his enemies (vs. 7b).**

- Levi: **Let your Thummim and Your Urim be with your holy one (vs. 6). Bless his substance, Lord, And accept the work of his hands; (vs. 11).**

- Benjamin: **The beloved of the Lord shall dwell in safety by Him, Who shelters him all the day long; And he shall dwell between his shoulders (vs. 12).**

- Joseph: **Blessed of the Lord is his hand, With the precious things of heaven and the dew (vs. 13).**

- Zebulun: **Rejoice, Zebulun, in your going out, And Issachar in your tents! (vs. 18).**

- Gad: **Blessed is he who enlarges Gad; (vs. 20).**

- Dan: **Dan is a lion's whelp; He shall leap from Bashan. (vs. 22).**

- Naphtali: **O Naphtali, satisfied with favor, And full blessing of the Lord, (vs. 23a).**

- Asher: **Asher is the most blessed of sons; Let him be favored by his brothers, And let him dip his feet in oil. (vs. 24).**

- Jeshurun: **The eternal God is your refuge, And underneath are the everlasting arms; (vs. 27).**

Therefore, we must dissect the origin of his humility, and apply that to our own lives. We must seek to know how Moses could have such a dramatic change of heart and mind. How could one be proud and arrogant when you had been face-to-face with Jehovah, the Creator, God Almighty? How could one be boastful when God calls you his friend? How could one brag and be condescending when you have been in the very presence of the glory and goodness of God. How can you live in anger when you have seen the goodness of God? You cannot possibly be anything but humble. Communion with God.

But again, how can you not be humble when your people and your family call you the greatest leader in all of Jewish history, and yet you know your own background from whence you came? You know you are not that magnificent? In your past, you have murdered your fellow man. You have ordered the destruction of your enemies and their children. You know you are not holy enough to be humble. In your relationship with others and with your own immediate family, you were not the best brother, the best husband, or the best father to your sons. Moses knew that God knew, and all of Israel knew.

However, Moses has grown and matured in both tenants of faith in which one loves God and loves his brother. He blessed those that did not bless him. He loved those that did not love him. He was not allowed to go into the "Promised Land" when others were allowed to go and yet he was comfortable with the outcome both spiritually and socially. He is complete: a man of humility.

He took the first commandment,

"You shall have no other Gods before Me,"
(Exodus 20:3)

and it became his "vision statement." He received from God and he revealed it to the Hebrew nation. He was blessed with God's glory and he showed the glory of God to the people, even so much so, that he had to have his face veiled so as to mask the brilliance of God's presence. He was God's handiwork made into the likeness of God in his humility. He was blessed and he blessed others. He belonged and knew

God in such closeness and intimacy, that God himself buried Moses on Mount Nebo. Born, blessed, and buried, all by God. A man who went from hostility to humility.

Application:

I do not know if I am the best person to address humility, for I find that I am anything but humble. Even as I write this book, I find myself asking if others will read it, will it be good as seen in the reader's eyes? Will it be successful? That is not humility and I know it. Therefore, we must now dig deeper, not into my thoughts, but into God's Word, and ask ourselves what humility means to God and how we too can be viewed as Moses was in his maturity and humility. How can we apply the principles we learned from Moses and apply them to our lives? The Bible tells us in 2 Chronicles 7:14,

"If My people who are called by My name will humble themselves, and pray and seek my face,

and turn from their wicked ways, then I will hear from heaven and forgive their sin and heal their land."

The Bible in Psalms tells us that God remembers the humble, he hears the humble, will make the humble glad, and will not forget the humble. In Isaiah 57:15, it reads,

"For thus says the High and Lofty One Who inhabits eternity, whose name is Holy: I dwell in the high and holy place, With him who has a contrite and humble spirit, To revive the spirit of the humble, And to revive the heart of the contrite ones."

Then in the New Testament both James and Peter quote from Proverbs and tells us that,

But He gives more grace. Therefore He says, "God resists the proud, but gives grace to the humble." (James 4:6).

and that we should be **"clothed with humility"** (I Peter 5:5a). It is not to the humiliated, but to the humble that God gives grace. Humility appears to activate God's favor and grace as he pours out blessings on those that seek only Him. Humility is the key to obtaining peace from men, peace from God, and peace within one's heart. But one of the keys to humility is not knowing who you are but knowing who God is. Teresa of Avila puts it this way,

"While we are on this earth nothing is more important than humility...In my opinion we shall never completely know ourselves if we don't strive to know God. By gazing at His grandeur, we get in touch with our lowliness; by looking at His purity, we shall see our own filth; by pondering His humility, we shall see how far we are from being humble." [13]

---

[13] Teresa of Avila, *The Interior Castle.* Sect. I, Chap. 2, no. 9, p. 292.

She continues on and comments that attachment from this world and humility always go together as "inseparable sisters." We are humble when we do not know it.

As one person pointed out, **"A proud person always thinks he's right. Humility is being able to say, 'I am wrong, and you are right,"** both to God and others. [14] Being right with God and others and being righteous are not the same, for Isaiah says,

But we are all like an unclean thing, And all our righteousnesses are like filthy rags; We all fade as a leaf, And our iniquities like the wind, Have taken us away." (Isaiah. 64:6).

What we appear to be and who God knows we are, can be quite a dichotomy. We are to be and act like the Bible tells us to be in Micah 6:8,

------

[14] Martin, R. (2006) *The Fulfillment of all Desire.* Steubenville, Ohio: Emmaus Road Publishing.

"He has shown you, O man, what is good; And what does the Lord require of you but to do justly, to love mercy, And to walk humbly with your God?

Again, it is the two-prong approach as we first discovered at the beginning of this chapter, for the **"do justly,** and **"to love mercy"** is directed to mankind, while to **"walk humbly"** is directed to God. Communion with God and community with Man. It takes both to be a whole, complete person with God and with man.

Mother Teresa, an Albanian by descent, spent her life caring for the poor in Calcutta, India has stated,

"I don't claim anything of the work. It's his work. I'm like a little pencil in his hand. That's all. He does the thinking. He does the writing. The pencil

has nothing to do with it. The pencil has only to be allowed to be used." [15]

We have come to see from the life of Moses that he was that pencil being used by God and being used by his fellowman. The closer he came to God, the closer he came to his fellow man. Humility is not a virtue, it is a relationship, and that is the lesson and its application to be learned. We cannot be humble; we are humble through the grace of God. God gives grace to the humble. (I Peter 5:5).

Humility

The state of being humble; freedom from pride and arrogance; a modest estimate of one's worth, or a sense of unworthiness through imperfection or sinfulness; lowliness; meekness; an opposite of pride, which may be regarded as the root and essence of sin. Humility is not to be regarded as

---

[15] Kelly-Gangi. (2006). *Mother Teresa Her Essential Wisdom.* New York, New York: Falls River Press. p. 61.

the root and essence of sin. Humility is not to be regarded as meanness or baseness, but it is a medium between foolish and ignominious self-effacement and vain glorying. The humble man does not attribute to himself any goodness or virtue that he does not possess, he does not overrate himself, he realizes his imperfections, and he ascribes all his goodness and good words to God's grace. The supreme example of humility is found in the incarnation and death of the Son of God. [16]

---

[16] Martin, W. (1964). *The Layman's Bible Encyclopedia.* Nashville, Tn.: The Southwestern Company, p. 332.

CHAPTER TWO

Elijah, the Prophet: From Depression to Deliverance

In James 5:17, it reads,

"Elijah was a man with a nature like ours, and he prayed earnestly that it would not rain; and it did not rain on the land for three years and six months."

A man with a nature like ours; a human nature, a regular man, a believer just like those that were being addressed by James, the half-brother of Jesus. It would appear that James was trying to say that normal people can do extraordinary things when joined together in the work of God. He had mentioned in the verses before,

"And the prayer of faith will save the sick, and the Lord will raise him up. And if he committed sins, they will be forgiven. Confess your trespasses to one another, and pray for one another, that you may be healed. The effective, fervent prayer of a righteous man avails much."

(James 5:15-16).

As you can see from the scriptures given, that if we pray, the Lord will raise us up, forgive our sins, and the relationship with God and man will be restored. Again, we are confronted with a two-prong approach to a mature walk with God: Communion with God and Community with Man. It is an Exodus replay.

There is no book of "Elijah" in the Old Testament, and he is not a prophet who wrote instructions down as other major and minor prophets did. In fact, we have only one written quote from Elijah and that is found in 2 Chronicles 21:12-15. The writer of Chronicles says that it is a letter to Jehoram from Elijah, but when put in historical perspective, Elijah had died or was translated by the whirlwind seven to thirteen years earlier. There is much dispute as to the nature and exactness of the letter and there has been no clear-cut answer as of yet. But as of now, that is all we know of Elijah's writings.

However, Elijah first comes on the scene in I Kings 17. He is looked upon in a similar vein as Moses, for he shows up at a time of great turmoil and during a great falling away from the faith of their fathers as the people turned to worshipping Baal and forsaking their God, Jehovah.

King Ahab and Queen Jezebel are reigning in power in Israel and they are considered as the most vile of all royalty that has ever ruled in Israel up until now. The Bible states,

"Now Ahab the son of Omri did evil in the sight of the Lord, more than all who were before him. And it came to pass, as though it had been a trivial thing for him to walk in the sins of Jeroboam the son of Nebat, that he took Jezebel the daughter of Ethbaal, king of the Sidonians; and he sent and served Baal and worshiped him."
(I Kings 16:30-31).

Elijah seemingly comes out of nowhere and begins his ministry in Israel and Judah. No history is given about his family or his faith, nor is there any earlier mention of him before I Kings 17. Elijah's name means, "Yahweh is my God," and he is

from Tishbi in Gilead. He is a "stranger from among the strangers in Gilead." (I Kings 17:1). He is alone, a rogue prophet, sent by God to the people to declare the Word of the Lord. We do not know if he has a family, a legacy, or a heritage from any lineage, except that he is from Gilead. We know that Gilead was known for its lush forests and green pastures, and for the production of "balm," which was a resin from a small tree that had healing properties. But Elijah is also called, Elijah the Tishbite, with the understanding that he is specifically from the town of Tishbeh which is also located in Gilead on the east side of the Jordan River. We know that he wore a garment of haircloth and a girdle of leather around his loin, but besides these few facts, we know little of Elijah except that he was a prophet called by God.

Later in the New Testament, with Moses representing the law, and Elijah representing the prophets, they will appear with Jesus on the Mount of Transfiguration. They are two men from the same mold: out of place, strangers or foreigners, aliens in a strange place, with no apparent family at this time, and with no friends either. Elijah is just beginning his ministry, and he will come later to understand who God is and who he is in relation to God and to man. Elijah is now actively working in the lives of the nation of Israel. He predicts a drought will occur and for three and a half years it did not rain, and then later he prayed for the end of the drought, and of course, the drought ended. Then in I Kings it tells of Elijah's miraculous feeding of the widow and then later of him bringing the widow's son back from the dead. He is prophesying and making predictions, interacting with kings and priests, until finally we come to the story most people may have heard of and that is, the confrontation with the prophets of Baal on Mount Carmel. As we are looking at Elijah and the Exodus replay of Moses, we will see some parallels of how God interacted in their lives.

Both Moses and Elijah will perform miracles at the hand of God, both will enter into a confrontation with the ruling elite, both will flee in fear and become depressed, and both will find help and solace in a new vision of God and in the brotherhood of believers.

Elijah enters into a contest with the prophets of Baal in I Kings 18 and on Mount Carmel they face off in a match about whose God will respond in a war of prayer. The prophets of Baal are followers of a god known by various names depending on the location and the needs of the people there. He is known as the sun god, the storm deity, the god of lightning, and a god who died and was resurrected with the passing cycles of nature as seen in the four seasons. Baal later comes to mean a generic name for the devil or evil no matter when or where he is manifested. In the New Testament, Jesus is even accused of casting our devils in the name of the devil, Baal- Ze bub.

Since Israel had no great rivers such as the Nile or Euphrates and relied solely on the needed rain that must come to bring prosperity to the country and its people, Israel was constantly asking, "Who sends the rain, Baal or Yahweh?" [17] Since Baal controls the weather, lightning, and the forces of nature, it is appropriate for Elijah to force a show down with the prophets of Baal on a mountain and call for an intervention by fire and a lightning bolt from heaven. Elijah set up the parameters of the conflict by placing two altars on top of Mount Carmel and then the prophets of Baal will call out first to their God, Baal, then Elijah will call out to Jehovah God and the people will see and know which God responds and is proclaimed as the God of Israel. The prophets of Baal set up the first altar of stone, place the sacrificial oxen and they begin their prayers and chants, with dancing and flagellation, but with no response by Baal. Elijah then follows with his altar of stone, with another ox slain, and then he proceeds to call out to God, Jehovah.

---

[17] Beaumont, M. (2012). *The New Lion Bible Encyclopedia*. Oxford, England: Lion Hudson Publishers.

I Kings records it this way,

"Hear me, O Lord, hear me, that this people may know that You are the Lord God, and that You have turned their hearts back to You again. Then the fire of the Lord fell and consumed the burnt sacrifice, and the wood and the stones and the dust, and licked up the water that was in the trench. Now when all the people saw it, they fell on their faces; and they said, "The Lord, He is God; The Lord, He is God!"
(I Kings 18:37-39).

In this story of the confrontation, Elijah is clearly the winner in this contest of Gods, and then he follows this miracle with another manifestation of God by calling on God and ending the drought. He is clearly the prophet of prophets, the man of the hour, the miracle maker.

However, Elijah like Moses, does not really understand the power that he possesses when he is in a right relationship with God, and in fear Elijah flees to the desert, as we read in I Kings 19:3a,

"And he was afraid and arose and ran for his life..."
(NASB).

Jezebel, the best-known evil woman of the Old Testament, and the wife of King Ahab threatens to kill Elijah, and Elijah ran. Then, in a "look what they are doing to me," moment, he not only runs, but he also hides. He has done this to himself, for it is not an outside force that forced him to run. It did not just happen to him. Jezebel was not stronger than Elijah and his God, but Elijah made a choice and chose fear over faith. We excuse Elijah for his behavior, for like many in the mental health profession, we conclude that people never, "will" their pathological behavior and are therefore not responsible for it. [18] But Elijah made a choice, and a wrong one at that.

Once again, like Moses, Elijah did not fully understand who God was, and Elijah as well, falls into the cycle of depression with loneliness, fear, sadness, anger, and depression. Before this flight into the wilderness, he had already declared the beginnings of this cycle of depression when he says,

"I alone am left a prophet of the Lord; but Baal's prophets are 450 men."
(I Kings 18:22).

Then in the next chapter he will declare this again a second time but under vastly different circumstances when he states,

So he said, "I have been zealous for the Lord God of hosts; for the children of Israel have forsaken

---

[18] Szasz, T. (1974). *The Myth of Mental Illness.* New York, New York: Harper and Row Publishers.

Your covenant, torn down Your altars, and killed Your prophets with the sword. I alone am left; and they seek to take my life."

Now he thinks he is alone socially and spiritually. He is away from his people, his family, his friends, and he thinks, his God. However, one must remember that loneliness is a choice and Elijah has made that choice. Loneliness has been with man since the beginning of time, when God in Genesis 2:18 says,

"And the Lord God said, "It is not good that man should be alone; I will make him a helper comparable to him."

We are social creatures and we need a relationship with God and with other people like ourselves. Nevertheless, this is where we find Elijah, feeling alone spiritually, socially, and in an emotional meltdown. The first time that Elijah declares his loneliness is as a "prophet" of God, in other words, he is saying I am alone with God as a prophet, as a called out one, as the lone representative of you. But then God intervenes in Elijah's time of depression and begins to clarify the facts for Elijah. Later Elijah will need to fill the people to people loss in his life as well.

One of the defining agents in depression is that one has inaccurate facts and that one interprets these facts in ways not founded in truth. but God is about to change these facts by giving a correct revelation to Elijah as to who Elijah is and who God is. Elijah is sitting in his desert cave and is pondering his predicament and God begins to interact with Elijah in ways he is unfamiliar with. I Kings 19:11 says,

"Then he said, "Go out, and stand on the mountain before the Lord." And behold the Lord passed by, and a great and strong wind tore into the mountains and broke the rocks to pieces before the Lord, but the Lord was not in the wind; and after the wind, an earthquake, but the Lord was not in the earthquake; and after the earthquake a fire, but the Lord was not in the fire: and after the fire a

still small voice. So it was, when Elijah heard it, that he wrapped his face in his mantle and went out and stood in the entrance of the cave. Suddenly a voice came to him, and said, "What are you doing here, Elijah?"

Elijah gets a new fresh vision of who God is and who he is not. The verse states that he is not in various manifestations of nature especially, fire, as seen in the confrontation with the prophets of Baal. Baal was tied to the worship of nature, but God, Jehovah, was above nature, above the realm of this world. God does not have to speak in power, he already has power, and therefore the still small voice is all that is needed to convey the revelation of who he is to Elijah and who Elijah is. In fact, it gives permission to Elijah to not have to be the strong prophet he thinks he must be if God himself does not have to react in fire and earthquakes. It lets Elijah realize that it is okay not to be strong as he conceives strength to be, but that he too may fail, he can be human, and he can also be godly at the same time. Is it not how loud you in the encounter, but how right and correct you are in the living out of that encounter. (Today in the Middle East, the person who is the loudest always wins the argument whether you are right or wrong, but that did not apply to this interaction.)

He is not in the abstract, in his created elements, but God is a personal God who speaks in a voice, a real voice, in language that you can understand and comprehend its meaning. Do not fear, do not be in despair, you are not alone. I am here and I am speaking with you. God is above what some call the "D" words; discouragement, doom, despair, defeat, and depression.

However, Elijah responds this time again with, **"I am alone,"** but he is not separated from God for he is talking to God face to face at that very moment. Elijah feels he is alone from others socially and he is needing a relationship with both God and man. God reminds him that there are seven thousand of his brothers in Israel that have not bowed down to Baal. He has a community of believers like himself that have the same nature as he does which reassures Elijah of his place in the nation. But it is like being in a crowd and still feeling lonely. You know the feeling when you go to the big social event, or you go to church and you stand there in the midst of believers, but no one knows you or recognizes you. You need more.

Elijah is exactly there, so he leaves his cave with the assurance that there is a God who speaks and there also is a community of seven thousand believers. However, he needs more! But there is more help on the way for Elijah and God through Elijah calls out Elisha in I Kings 19:19,

So he departed from there, and found Elisha the son of Shaphat, who was plowing with twelve yokes of oxen before him, and he was with the twelfth. Then Elijah passed by him and threw his mantle on him. (I Kings 19:19).

From this point on, Elijah has a helper, a friend, a co-worker, a companion, that will nurture him. He has a God who speaks and seven thousand friends of Jehovah, and now a personal friend who cares.

How do we know Elisha cares for his mentor? Elisha becomes his servant and later when Elijah is being called up into heaven, Elijah tells Elisha,

"Stay here, please, for the Lord has sent me on to the Jordon." But he (Elisha) said to him, "As the Lord lives, and your soul lives, I will not leave you." So, the two of them went on. (2 Kings 2:6).

Elisha saw what Proverbs 18:24b alludes to:

"But there is a friend that sticks closer than a brother."

Elisha stayed with Elijah to the very end of Elijah's existence on this earth. He was there and he was listening.

So, can you too beat the depressive nature of Elijah's life? Yes, you can, for Elijah, as stated at the first of this chapter was a man of like nature with us, but he also was a man nurtured by his God, his friends, and his community. It is not nature vs nurture; it is nature and nurture. They are both needed to be a mature believer, a complete person, whole, and in our right mind.

As noted in the story of Moses and in this story of Elijah, we must have a valid, strong relationship with our creator, our savior, our Lord, but at the same time, we must have a valid, strong relationship with our community and our friends. Communion with God and Community with Man.

Community does not mean that we are living in a stable world of fellowship and freedom and spend all of our time, "breaking bread." Elijah and Moses were not spending their time just playing golf and eating Nachos. They were in a life of conflict, a life that needed a firm relationship with God and man. They were in the midst of social turmoil, corruption, with a people ignorant of the things of God. They, and we too, need to spend time in fellowship with God and with man. It needs to be more than just church, we need each other, both with the good and those that are seeking to be better.

Martin Luther wrote,

"The Kingdom is to be in the midst of your enemies. And he who will not suffer this does not want to be of the Kingdom of Christ; he wants to be among friends, to sit among roses and lilies, not with the bad people but the devout people. O you blasphemers and betrayers of Christ! If Christ had done what you are doing who would have been spared."

This "Kingdom of God" is an active and not a static or localized concept, and could be better translated as "rule, reign," not "kingdom." [19] We are looking not for a personalized experience per se, but we are looking for Christ to reign collectively over the

---

[19] Brown, R. (1984). *The Churches the Apostles Left Behind*. Mahwah, New Jersey: Paulist Press, p. 51.

entire world. We want a community of believers that seek to be ruled by God.

Dietrich Bonhoeffer, the renowned Christian martyr of World War II, longed for that community and fellowship with both God and man. He wrote,

"The believer feels no shame, as though he is still living too much in the flesh, when he yearns for the physical presence of other Christians. Man was created a body, the Son of God appeared on earth in the body, he was raised in the body, in the sacrament the believer receives the Lord Christ in body, and the resurrection of the dead will bring about the perfected fellowship of God's spiritual-physical creatures. The believer lauds the Creator, the Redeemer, God, Father, Son and Holy Spirit, for the bodily presence of a brother.... It is grace,

nothing but grace, that we are allowed to live in community with Christian brethren. [20]

Bonhoeffer went on to say, **"Christian brotherhood is not an ideal which we must realize, it is rather a reality created by God in Christ in which we may participate." [21]**

Elijah in his depression got a fresh glimpse of God and through Elisha, Elijah got a fresh glimpse of community and the friendship of man. May we also get both. Elijah has gone from despair and depression to being delivered. Deliverance is defined as being released from bondage, danger, or evil of any kind; set free: to deliver one from slavery. [22]He has been set free. He is not alone.

---

[20] Bonhoeffer, D. (1954). *Life Together*, New York, New York: Harper One, pp. 19-20.

[21] Ibid, pp. 30.

[22] Morris, W. (1976). *The American Heritage Dictionary of the English Language*. Boston, Mass.: Houghton Mifflin Company.

"If we walk in the light as He is in the light, we have fellowship with one another, and the blood of Jesus Christ His Son cleanses us from all sin."

(I John 1:7)

It is interesting that Elijah prayed to die and God did not answer his prayer, but did the exact opposite and today, almost 3500 years later, Elijah is still alive and has never faced death since his miraculous move to heaven by a whirlwind. He went from depression to deliverance and beyond. Later, in the end times, he will come again before the return of Christ and be instrumental in fulfilling all that was prophesied in both the Old and New Testaments.

Deliverance

Deliverance is to be set free from sin and the evil one. To be liberated from death and the worries that come with being burdened with sin. To release one to find peace and safety in the hands of our Lord. To be rescued and delivered into the hands of our savior as one who would be delivered

in childbirth to the parents that hold a newborn child so dear. To be released to be all that God meant you to be. To find that those things that bound you bind you no more. To be set free as one who had been set free from slavery. The act of being taken out of danger and surrendering to God's will. To be delivered from fears (Psalm 34:4), from trouble (Psalm 54:7), and from the power of darkness (Col. 1:13).

Application:

In Elijah's classic diagnosis of depression, we want to examine its origin and to reconstruct the problem. Proverbs 23:7 says, **"For as he thinks in his heart, so is he."** This scripture has been the basis of many psychological therapies and much discussion on the nature of man. If we look back we can see the ideas presented in this scriptures in the development of Alcoholic Anonymous with its, "stinking thinking," or with Rational Emotive Behavior Therapy, with its ABC's of therapy where A is the situation, B is the thoughts, and C is the Feelings or Actions. Cognitive Behavior Therapy and many more therapeutic systems are just a renaming of old ideas packaged in new terminology. It is because in all therapy, our ultimate goal is not just to change behavior, but to change one's thinking that causes the aberrant behavior.

In a nutshell it goes like this:

For example, you are angry and upset and you need to learn how to control or rid yourself of this anger that is focused onto a situation. A is the situation that you are angry about, for example, let us say your spouse. He/She is late for an appointment. B is the thought about the lateness and your demands about the situation. You think they was negligent in their timeliness, therefore you reacted with anger, the C, or the feelings about their timeliness. We think that A, the situation, causes C, the anger, when really B, the thinking about the lateness, caused the anger. We then proceed to breakdown the thinking making suggestions as to the nature of the lateness and the anger. Maybe your spouse had a flat tire and was late for that reason. Maybe your spouse was sick and had to go to the doctor and that is why they never showed up for the appointment. Once you clarify B, the thinking, then you can change C, the anger. [23]

It is a simplified explanation of REBT or CBT, but many psychologists would argue that the therapy is not that easy or simple, but in reality it is unbelievably simple and it has its origins in Proverbs 23:7, **"As a man thinketh, so is he,"** and it is quite exact in its explanation.

In this application, is where we find Elijah, for he had really inaccurate thought processes because he had a lack of real exact information. Elijah became depressed for he thought he was alone, the first step to depression, when in actuality there were seven thousand people that were united with him against

---

[23] Hafner, A. (2002). *Anger.* Center City, Mn.: Hazelden Press, p. 9.

the corrupt regime of Ahab the king. He thought he was alone, but he was not. That was the main problem at the beginning of his depression and despair. He did not have all the facts in the correct order of events.

Loneliness is the heartbeat of depression, whether it is alone without God, or alone without man. Depression is one of the greatest psychological problems of today and at the top of the list for today's maladies. Surrounded by the masses we feel alone like going to a party and finding you are the only one wearing a tie in the midst of the crowd. You wish that you had just one person who cared and also wore a tie. You fear no one knows you or acknowledges you and you become moody and angry, spiteful, and worried. Am I the only one? Why am I living if no one even cares for me? What is life without friends and family? Why doesn't anyone want to reach out to me?

Pastor Jim Baker of PTL fame in his book, *"The Refuge"* (2000) relates in the chapter, *"One Really is the Loneliest Number"* the following story:

"I spent five years living with hundreds of men in federal prisons, in an environment that provided little privacy. We were constantly exposed to the incessant (and frequently grotesque) noise and activity of prison life. Now wonder by the time I reached the farm in North Carolina, I was ready for some solitude, peace, and quiet.

But then a surprising thing happened. As I slowly became accustomed to real "life on the outside," I discovered that I was extremely lonely. Jim Baker lonely? The man who had preached to millions of people around the world- lonely? A fellow who once had to have security guards just to be able to relax in his home due to the constant press of people- lonely?

It was true. No matter what I did, I could not shake the awful feelings of isolation that dogged me night and day.

I enjoyed the opportunities that solitude provided to spend time with God, to study his Word, to pray, sometimes just walking around the house talking aloud to Him, sometimes sitting in the yard, contemplating the beautiful, natural setting around me. But I was alone." [24]

Elijah as seen in the previous chapter, was more than feeling alone. He was physically tired, emotionally drained, exhausted, in fear of his life, and alone as well. He finds a broom tree and sits down and tells God to **"Take my life."** (I Kings 19:4). Elijah is in bad shape spiritually, socially, mentally, and he is suicidal as well. He has incorrect thinking about the situation he is in. He had been doing the work of the prophet, but he was alone. He had been praying and

---

[24] Baker, J. (2000). *The Refuge*. Nashville, TN.: Thomas Nelson Publishers, p. 39.

calling out to God, but he still felt alone. He had all the classic symptoms of depression: 1. Depressed or irritable mood, 2. Diminished interest or pleasure in all, or almost all activities, 3. Significant weight loss or weight gain, or significant increase or decrease in appetite, 4. Insomnia, excessive sleeping, or other sleep problems, 5. Physical restlessness or slowed body movement, 6. Fatigue or loss of energy, 7. Feelings of worthlessness; excessive of inappropriate guilt, 8. Diminished ability to think, concentrate, or make decisions.[25]

He had all the wrong thoughts in all the wrong places.

Rick Warren in his book, "God's Answers to Life's Difficult Questions," states,

---

[25] Ingersoll, B., Goldstein, S. (1995). *Lonely, Sad, and Angry, A Parent's Guide to Depression in Children and Adolescents.* New York, New York: Doubleday, pp. 5-10.

"If you think in a negative way, you are going to feel depressed. Your emotions are caused by how you interpret life. If you look at life from a negative viewpoint, you're going to get down.

If you want to get rid of negative emotions, you have to change the way you think. The Bible says that you must be transformed by the *renewing of your mind* (Rom.12:2). To overcome depression, you must get your incorrect attitudes about life corrected. [26]

Elijah thought he was alone, but he was not, for there were thousands by his side. Elijah thought God had left him, but God had not. God was still speaking to him in a still, quiet voice. Elijah thought no one knew his whereabouts, but God knew exactly where he was and came with a visitation of his presence. Elijah was physically hungry, and he thought he had no provisions, but God provided food and drink for

---

[26] Warren, R. (2006). *God's Answers to Life's Difficult Questions*. Grand Rapids, MI.: Zondervan. p. 45.

him. Elijah thought he had no one to help him or befriend him, but God sent Elisha his way, and Elisha never left Elijah's side.

Again, we must emphasize that those in depression have an inaccurate interpretation of the events unfolding in one's life and Elijah surely was confused as to the facts of the matter. He needed clarification and he got it from God and from his new companion and friend, Elisha.

Again, as we have emphasized over and over again. You must have "Communion with God," and "Community with Man." Elijah was reformed and renewed because both areas of change agents happened and restored him to a right relationship with God and man.

Rabbi Harold Kushner author of *Why Bad Things Happen to Good People* (1981) said in an interview:

Do you want to feel good about yourself? Be part of a community of people who are dedicated to

doing good. It's not easy to be the only person in your crowd that pays his taxes honestly. It's not easy to be the only person in your group who refrains from malicious gossip. Find yourself a sub-community, a sub-set of people who believe what you believe… Bounce off each other; reinforce each other; encourage each other. This is what churches and synagogues do. You don't go to church to become a good person. You become a good person, you go to church; you surround yourself with good people. You have values and your commitments reinforced. You don't have this sense that, "I'm out of step with the community; everybody else is trying to get their own thing, to fill their own pockets, and I'm the only lonely saint out here." Just the opposite. You find that you are part of God's army and it becomes a lot easier to do it when people around you are doing it. [27]

------

[27] Kushner, H. (1981). *When Bad Things Happen to Good People.* New York, New York: Anchor Books.

Communion and Community will solve many of life's problems, so implement strategies that work and reinforce them in your life and see what God can do. He did it for Moses, and he did it for Elijah, and he can do it for you. Elijah now had God and he also had his companion and friend, Elisha. He went from depression to deliverance. Now come with me in chapter three and see how God did it for John, the apostle, as well.

John, the Apostle: From Arrogance to Authenticity

John the apostle, John the disciple, John the evangelist, or John the revelator are all names for the same man that we will explore in this chapter. John was one of the sons of Zebedee and the brother to James, who were both fishermen from Galilee. He was in business with Peter and Andrew in the fishing industry, but later

John would quit fishing to become a follower of Jesus. He had been an earlier disciple of John the Baptist along with Andrew, his friend and fellow apostle. John lived the longest of any disciple, dying at the age of 93-94 in A.D. 100 in the city of Ephesus, which is located in present day Turkey. He was very prominent in the ministry with Jesus and he was there at Jesus' first tour into Galilee. He owned a home in Jerusalem and was a prominent citizen of the time and was widely known in religious circles. He wrote the Gospel of John, the three Epistles of John, and the Book of Revelation. John was one of the inner three of Peter, James, and John that Jesus called upon to assist him in various ministry functions. He was one of the twelve that was sent out on a preaching ministry. He seemed to be at every main event that is recorded in the Gospels.

John was there at the wedding in Cana, and he was present on the first tour of ministry into Galilee. He was one of the three disciples at the Transfiguration of Jesus. He is the only gospel writer to talk of the raising of Lazarus, the meeting of the Samaritan woman, the washing of the disciples feet, as well as the doubting Thomas incident. He was present at the raising of Jairus' daughter, was sent to prepare the Passover meal, and at that meal, the Last Supper, he took the place of privilege at the head of the table, next to Jesus. He was the only disciple that was at the cross and was given the command to take care of Mary, the mother of Jesus. He was with Peter during the time of Jesus' burial, and then again with Peter as one of the first visitors to the empty tomb after the resurrection of Jesus. John wrote what some call the "spiritual gospel" and was an early church father and a pastor of the Church of Ephesus. According to John's gospel, John was the "apostle" of the apostles and was called,

"the disciple whom Jesus loved."
(John 19:26)

However, it is in light of this last phrase, **"the disciple whom Jesus loved,"** that John's original personality begins to reveal itself. And this is where we see the problem; his personal ego, his vanity, and his pride start to be made manifested. You must understand that he is the author of the book of John and in five different scriptures he calls himself, **"the disciple whom Jesus loved."** Now if Matthew or the other gospel writers always make mention of John in this most privileged position then we could excuse it, but that is not the case. John alone mentions that he is "it." He is the one, the important one. He also tells of how he went with Peter to the tomb of Jesus and as if is important, he says that he, John, outran Peter, got there first, and looked into the tomb before Peter. He also said that he looked into the tomb and believed. (John 20).

We again saw this in his personality in his ministry with Jesus when John in his zeal, intolerance, and his feelings of exclusiveness rebuked a man because he was casting our demons and he was not one of the twelve disciples. (Mark 3:17). Earlier John also wanted to call down fire from heaven on a

Samaritan village because they refused to serve the disciples food and they did not receive Christ into their village with any kind of welcome (Luke 9:54). John and his brother, James, earned the name, "Sons of Thunder" as nicknames of rebuke for their insolence and shameless pride. John, as recorded in Mark 10 asks,

"Teacher, we want You to do for us whatever we ask." And He said to them, "What do you want Me to do for you?" They said to Him, "Grant us that we may sit on Your right hand and the other on Your left, in your glory."

Jesus proceeds to rebuke the brothers again and even the disciples are greatly displeased with John and James. He may have had a good Communion with God, but his Community with Man was not quite as it should be. John was a man of great ego not realizing as in the title of the book by Ryan Holiday that, *"Ego is the enemy,"* (2016). Holiday states,

"Christians believe that pride is a sin because it is a lie – it convinces people that they are better than they are, that they are better than God made them. Pride leads to arrogance and then away from humility and connection with their fellow man." [28]

For John that was his problem for his ambition, ego, pride, and vanity ran rampant through the gospels. Even at the Last Supper, John records that in a conversation between Peter and Jesus, Peter has to go through John to get an audience with Jesus, and John is the go between or the arbitrator for the group. He mentions that it is the disciple who Jesus loved, again speaking of himself.

Now there was leaning on Jesus' bosom one of His disciples, whom Jesus loved. Simon Peter therefore motioned to him to ask who it was of whom He spoke. Then leaning back on Jesus' breast, he said to Him, "Lord, who is it?"

---

[28] Holiday, R. (2016). *Ego is the Enemy*. New York, New York: Penguin Random House Publishers. p. 74.

(John 13:23-25).

John, it appears, is full of himself, his own ego.

We next find John in Acts 3, where he, along with Peter, are at the healing of the lame man at the Gate of the Temple. However, this time the writer of Acts, Luke, records that Peter is the person in charge, not John.

Now Peter and John went up together to the temple at the hour of prayer, the ninth hour, And a certain man lame from his mother's womb was carried, whom they laid daily at the edge of the temple which is called Beautiful, to ask for alms from those who entered the temple, who, seeing Peter and John about to go into the temple asked for alms. And fixing his eyes on him, with John, Peter said, "Look at us." So he gave them his attention, expecting to receive something from them. Then Peter said, "Silver and gold I do not have, but what I do have I give you: In the name of

Jesus Christ of Nazareth, rise up and walk." (Acts 3:1-6).

I wonder what John would have wrote if he had been recording this incident? We will never know, but I am sure he would place himself in the leadership position.

Later in the next chapter, John and Peter are arrested and in the following scripture portions, it lists the personalities in the story as Peter and John, with Peter being the one recognized as the leader in the forefront. John when not writing about himself does not seem to occupy the significance that earlier he gave himself.

Even in Galatians 2:9, when Paul writes about defending the Gospel, he notes that, **"James, Cephas, and John who seem to be pillars, perceived the grace...."** He does not say they are the pillars of faith or of the church, but that they seem to be just that. John is not quite the man he arrogantly thought he once was. Soon events in his life are going to change him in ways that he never thought possible. His entire personality is going to change and change for the better. Let us now continue to identify the life changes that will emerge in his ministry and effect his attitude that will purge John to become who he really is and for the purpose God appointed him to be.

According to tradition, John moved to Ephesus shortly before the destruction of Jerusalem in A.D. 70, and became the pastor of the church there. He also had a special relationship with the other churches in the area, serving as a "bishop" or lead pastor, both before exile to Patmos and after. While living in Ephesus, John had Mary, the mother of Jesus, living with him and he cared for her until her death. Today in Ephesus, one can visit Mary's house, or so it is rumored. It has not been substantiated, but many say it is the place where she later died. No archaeological evidence of Mary's tomb has actually been found in Ephesus and the exact location of her tomb is still in debate. However, according to St. Irenaeus, John did live in Ephesus and Mary as well until the time of Trajan. [29]

But now, history and the life of John takes a turn for the worst with the death of his brother, James. James, John's brother, was the first to die in martyrdom in Jerusalem, with all the other disciples dying violently as well in the near future. But John was the only apostle who never died a martyr's death and died peacefully in Ephesus at the age of 93-94.

---

[29] McBirnie, W. (1977). *The Search for the Twelve Apostles*. Wheaton, Illinois: Tyndale Publishing House.

Library Façade in Ephesus

He was living in Ephesus when Domitian, the Roman Emperor in the year of AD 51-96, declared himself to be a God, and John in opposition rose up against this proclamation which brought on his arrest and later his exile to the Isle of Patmos in A.D. 94. Before Domitian's proclamation Christians were regarded as a sect of Judaism and were tolerated, but later when Rome understood that Christianity was a new religion, Christianity lost its legal security and upon that fact, Domitian was able to react with violent acts of persecution towards the Church of Ephesus. Ephesus was one of the centers of Christian activity, with Paul, Timothy, John, and Mary residing there thus giving it prominence in early church development. Paul, later when imprisoned in Rome, addresses one of his letters to the Church in Ephesus, known to us as the Book of Ephesians.

Ephesus at this time had a temple to the Roman Emperor Domitian that was built on the highest promenade of Ephesus which today is called, Nightingale Hill. You can visit the remains of this temple which lie next to the upper agora, which in contrast to the lower agora or market, this upper agora was strictly for government duties. All that was found during recent archaeological excavations of the Domitian Temple site was the head and an arm of Emperor Domitian. It is said that,

"Domitian had a deep sense of inferiority, the result, no doubt, of being constantly overshadowed by a dominant father and a brilliant elder brother; and he lived in a morbid terror of being supplanted. It was to offset his sense of insecurity that he began to demand towards the end of his reign that his subjects should worship him as god."[30]

The temple in Ephesus to Domitian is built on top of and supported by columns of other gods' statues, giving the message that the Emperor Domitian was a god in a position of power over all the other gods of the time. He even towered over Artemis or Diana, the patron god of Ephesus. Her temple occupied a position in a lower area of the city and all that remains today of that great wonder of the world, is one lone column in a watery marsh.

---

[30] *Dominus et Deus*: see Dio Cassius lxvii. 13; Suetonius, *Dom.* 13; Martial v.8.

Ephesus was a neokorate, or a city dedicated to the imperial cult of Rome and in this case, it was dedicated to Domitian. There was a fifty-foot-tall statue of the Emperor Domitian in the city and besides Nero, who had ruled earlier, Domitian was the most aggressive persecutor of Christians of his time. Even if one had to go to shop or conduct business in the agora in Ephesus, all entering had to place incense and offerings into an incense burner placed at the agora's entrance, which again was dedicated to the worship of Domitian. In Roman rule, one kept the empire together by having a common God to worship, with that again being the Emperor, thus assuring him of your loyalty. Because John stood in opposition to the worship of Domitian, and because of the general persecution of all Christians by Domitian, John was exiled to the island of Patmos, which is a small island off the coast of what was then known as Asia Minor.

The Isle of Patmos today is a Greek island forty miles off the coast of Turkey. [31] Some say John was not just exiled but it was a case of *deportatio in insulam,* which is a penalty that not only exiled you, but confiscated all of your personal property and took away any civil rights that one may have secured then and in the years that followed.

The Isle of Patmos was a prison island, but not with your typical prison or jail cells, as one would think, for the prisoners were not confined in solitary confinement but it was more of a penal colony of criminals that would work as slaves and would be guarded by the Romans as they labored. John was thought to have been placed there as a prisoner to process the salt from the salt flats on the island, but later evidence seems to refer to his ability to freely roam the island at will. Exiled, but not totally bound. By tradition it is said that John lived in a cave, which

---

[31] Stowell, J. (2020). *Seven Churches of Revelation.* Day of Discovery Television Series.

can still be viewed today. He lived for about two years on the Island of Patmos, until the death of Emperor Domitian, at which time he returned to live in Ephesus. The cave, or grotto, on Patmos and the indention of where John is said to have rested his head is now viewed as a valuable relic and is protected in the Monastery of the Apocalypse that is run by Byzantine monks. The cave, which is within the monastery compound, is reported to be the very cave where John received the last book of the Bible, The Revelation. Today the island and the cave, called the Cave of the Apocalypse, is a place of pilgrimage where Christians come by the thousands to view the place where Jesus revealed this book of mysteries to John, the Revelator. Today the cave's stone roof of natural rock is cracked in three places signifying the trinitarian nature of God who appeared and spoke to John at this very spot. Much of this historical fact is open to speculation, but the Isle of Patmos is still a fascinating place to visit and to understand the nature of John and his personal encounter with God.

It is here where the story of the transformation of John begins. It is where John has a change of heart and a change of direction. You remember from the preceding paragraphs and the Gospel of John, that John was a vain man, full of himself, and full of pride. He was the "disciple who Jesus loved," as attested by no less than John himself. At the point of his exile to Patmos, John had already written the Gospel of John with his favorable impression of himself, however, Jesus is now going to reveal to John a picture of himself that will totally reconstruct John's vision of Jesus and of John himself.

Revelation chapter one, verse 9 begins,

"I, John, both your brother and companion in the tribulation and kingdom and patience of Jesus Christ, was on the island that is called Patmos for the word of God and for the testimony of Jesus Christ. I was in the Spirit on the Lord's Day, and I heard behind me a loud voice,, as of a trumpet, saying, "I am the Alpha and the Omega, the First

and the Last," and, "What you see, write in a book and send it to the seven churches which are in Asia: to Ephesus, to Smyrna, to Pergamos, to Thyatira, to Sardis, to Philadelphia, and to Laodicea."

Then I turned to see the voice that spoke with me. And having turned I saw seven golden lampstands One like the Son of Man, clothed with a garment down to the feet and girded about the chest with a golden band. His head and hair were white like wool, as white as snow, and His eyes like a flame of fire; His feet were like fine brass, as if refined in a furnace, and His voice as the sound of many waters; He had in His right hand seven stars, out of His mouth went a sharp two-edged sword, and His countenance was like the sun shining in its strength. And when I saw Him, I fell at his feet as dead. But He laid His right hand on me, saying to me, "Do not be afraid; I am the First and the Last. I am He who lives, and was dead, and behold, I am alive forever more. Amen." (Revelation 1:9-18a).

John, who once asked to be seated on Jesus' right hand in heaven, now could not even lift his head. John, who asked for fire to be sent down from heaven and consume the Samaritan village, was now consumed with fear at the sight of the majesty of Jesus, the Christ. It was not like the Jesus of the Cross, nor the Jesus of the resurrection, but this was the Jesus of the God head seen here in all his glory and splendor. The Book of Revelation says that, John was as a dead man. He had finally had a true vision of Christ, the Christ of all eternity. Christ was there in his power. Christ was there in his magnificence. Christ was touching both heaven and earth with stars in his hands and power in his presence. He is standing in the midst of the golden lampstands, which is the first characteristic of Christ revealed to John in this vision. He is showing John that he is present among the earthly congregations of his people. Jesus is wearing the garb of the high priest with a robe and a girdle. He has the white hair, a mark of the Ancient of Days, along with bronze feet to remind us of Ezekiel's cherubim. He has the voice of returning glory as seen in Ezekiel 43:2. [32]

John is totally out of his comfort zone and is experiencing Christ like he has never understood him to be. He once saw Christ in a similar way on the Mount of Transfiguration when Jesus was changed into his heavenly glory in front of Peter, James, and John. However, John at that time did not deem it important as he does not record it in his gospel when the others all do. He just did not "get it" at the time when the very manifestation of heavenly things was being revealed at the transfiguration, but now, this was way more than a mere change of clothes and a brightness of face. This event at the start of the Book of Revelation was too wonderful to explain or to understand, and John from this moment on is a changed man. The Bible records in verse one of

---

[32] Caird, G. (1966). *A Commentary of The Revelation of St. John the Divine.* New York, NY.: Harper and Row Publishers, p. 25.

Revelation that this was, **"The Revelation of Jesus Christ..."** This was not just a revelation of things to come but it was also a revelation as to the nature of God himself. Revelation means to "take the cover off" or *apokalupsis* which is from the preposition *apo*, from, and *kalupto,* to cover. It is the uncovering of the glory of Christ and of what the future holds. [33]

John is overwhelmed and falls down at Christ's feet as if he is dead. John has seen Christ like no one had seen him before. John is in exile and with time on his hand and a change in his heart, he is ready to listen. Like Moses who turned aside to hear the voice in the burning bush, and like Elijah who listened to the still small voice of God, John too is listening to the voice like the sound of many waters. He is ready for the Revelation of Jesus Christ. John is changed forever both in Spirit and in his personality.

---

[33] Zodhiates, S. (1977). *The Hebrew-Greek Key Study Bible.* Chattanooga, Tn.: AMG Publishers.

How do we know John is forever different? Take a look at the John of the Gospel that was written earlier (The oldest manuscript from the New Testament is a fragment of the Gospel of John written between 100-140 A.D. and is on display in the John Rylands Library in Manchester, England). Then compare the John of the gospel to the John of the three Epistles of John. The epistles were written after his understanding of who Jesus is in Revelation and he writes and communicates in a totally different way and with a personality that is rooted in Christ and others, not himself. He goes from the "disciple whom Jesus loved," to just calling himself the "Elder." He appears to be saying, "I am just the old man who on the Isle of Patmos and got a fresh revelation of who Jesus is and it is more than you can even imagine. I have the images in my head, but I cannot even explain them in terms that you can understand. I know Jesus, and this is what I have seen and heard." He is hearing Jesus and he is writing it all down, even though it is beyond his comprehension.

John writes in his epistles,

But if we walk in the light as He is in the light, we have fellowship with one another, the blood of Jesus Christ His son cleanses us from all sin. (I John 1:7).

He who says he is in the light, and hates his brother, is in darkness until now. (I John 2:9).

For all that is in the world – the lust of the flesh, the lust of the eyes, and the pride of life – is not of the Father but is of the world. (I John 2:16).

By this we know love, because He laid down His life for us. And we also ought to lay down our lives for the brethren. (I John 3:16).

Beloved, let us love one another, for love is of God, and everyone who loves is born of God and knows God. (I John 4:7).

If someone says, "I love God," and hates his brother, he is a liar; for he who does not love his brother who he has seen, how can he love God

who he has not seen. And this commandment we have from Him: that he who loves God must love his brother also. (I John 4:20-21.

As you read these epistles and the scriptures that mention love over a hundred times in one way or another, you realize that this is not the arrogant John of the gospels. John has met the Jesus of the Revelation and he now knows who he is and who God is. John has changed and he has changed for the betterment of the church. He talks of love for God and love for man. He talks of living a life of compassion and has lost the edge of the old John. John is an older, wiser, and more mature man in the Lord, and it shows in all he writes.

John sees things in himself and others that he makes mention of in his epistles. In psychology we understand that those things we easily recognize in others is probably that which is easily seen in us. I have seen that manifested in Alcoholic Anonymous meetings where those that know addiction can easily see those that are trying to hide behind false pretenses. Every old addict can easily spot someone that is being untruthful. They know instinctively because they have been there and have been on the same path.

John is also there, not in addiction, but in calling out what he knows within himself. In the Third Epistle of John, John calls out a church member, Diotrephes for his arrogance. John writes,

I wrote to the church, but Diotrephes, who loves to have the preeminence among them, does not receive us. Therefore, if I come, I will call to mind his deeds which he does, prating against us with malicious words...
(3 John 1:9-10)

Diotrephes sounds a lot like the old John to me, the one who always wanted to be first, to sit at the right hand of Jesus, to call fire down from heaven on the Samaritans, and to rebuke those that did not do what he, John, thought was right. John called it as he knew it and Diotrephes was acting out in a similar fashion. John had himself been there in the past, and he recognized that this attitude was not of God and would destroy the church. But now John was changed because he had been with Jesus in all his glory, and just like Moses and Elijah, he had looked, listened, and learned. The old John now could compare and contrast who he was and could also recognize it in Diotrephes as well.

David Jeremiah writes in his commentary on Third John,

The great English preacher Charles Spurgeon once said, "A man who will not do well in his present place because he longs to be higher is already too high and should be put lower." The self-seeking and self-important Diotrephes heads a long line of people who never learned to distinguish between the love for Christ and love for their place in the church... Today, we find such an attitude

manifested in churches that become a cult of personality. Those with "Diotrephes Disease" want to be first; they greedily seek prominence and control. Yet one person can have preeminence among God's people: Christ (Col. 1:18). [34]

John did have "Diotrephes Disease" but was cured by the fresh revelation of God. He was cured of his arrogance and he became authentic and grew into humility.

Jerome, an early church father, tells us that John in his later years could not walk and had to be carried around in the arms of other disciples and believers from the church in Ephesus. He was elderly and did not talk much but when he did, all he said was, "Little children, love one another." After some time, the community of believers got tired of hearing the same thing over and over and asked John one day, "Master, why do you always say this?" "It is the Lord's

---

[34] Jeremiah, D. (2013). *The Jeremiah Study Bible.* Nashville, TN.: Worthy Publishing.

command," he replied. "And if this alone be done, it is enough." John, the "Apostle of Love," understood that the greatest command as taught by Jesus was all that one needs to do: "Love God and love your neighbor." He understood that we must have Communion with God and Community with Man, and John lived in an authentic expression of that in words and deeds.

John goes on to live until the reign of Nerva, 68 years after the resurrection of Jesus, and he served the church at Ephesus as pastor and bishop until his death. After his death, he was buried in Ephesus and a small church was built over the tomb of John and it later became a place of pilgrimage, so much so, that in the 6th century Emperor Justinian erected the Basilica of Saint John over the remains of the older smaller church to accommodate the masses that came to pay homage to the last of the twelve apostles. Today, one can still visit the ruins of this church in Ephesus and see the monograms of Emperor

Justinian and his wife Theodora emboldened on the restored columns of the church. [35]

According to tradition, John is buried under the part of the floor that is under the large dome on the east side of the church. One can also see the baptistery located on the north side of the church. The church is formally laid out in the form of a cross in honor of the memory of Jesus and his crucifixion. The church is in disrepair, but the memory of John is still alive to the many pilgrims who visit his tomb and remember his life and his love.[36] He went from arrogance to authenticity and it is recognized by seekers of God that today still pay homage to this, "Beloved Disciple."

---

[35] Camci, M. *Ephesus*. Istanbul, Turkey: Alas Ticaret ve Basim Sanayi

[36] McBirnie, W. (1977). *The Search for the Twelve Apostles*. Wheaton, Illinois: Tyndale Publishing House.

Authenticity

Authenticity is to be free from falsehoods about God, yourself, and others. It is to be genuine in mind and spirit. To be trustworthy in your relationship with God and in your relationship with mankind. To be true, honest, and reliable, and original in your beliefs. You are to be as you say you are and to act as you say you will act. You are the same to all, whether it is to the alien living among you, or the enemy that confronts you at every turn. You are to be family to those that have not experienced inherent authority. Authenticity is not knowing how we see ourselves or how others see us, but authenticity is living in the way and nature of how God sees us.

2 Corinthians 1:12 tells us to boast in this: "the testimony of our conscience that we conducted ourselves in the world in simplicity and godly sincerity, not with fleshly wisdom but by the grace of God, and more abundantly toward you."

Application:

In the application of humility and the changes in the spiritual and in the emotional-psychological life of John, I am sure he did not find this application to be an easy fit. He had been taught how to behave from early childhood and from his parents he had learned many things and he applied them to his own life. You may remember that John's mother approached Jesus asking for privileged positions for her two sons, James, and John. In Matthew 20 it reads,

Then the mother of the sons of Zebedee came to Him with her sons, bowing down, and making a request of Him. And He said to her, "What do you wish?" She said to Him, "Command that in Your kingdom these two sons of mine may sit, one on Your right and one on Your left." But Jesus answered and said, "You do not know what you are asking for. Are you able to drink the cup that I am about to drink?" They said, "We are able." He said to them, "My cup you shall drink; but to sit on

My right and on My left, this is not Mine to give, but it is for those whom it has been prepared by the Father." (Matthew 20:20-23.)

As you can see, John learned some invaluable lessons on life from his mother. John's mother was bold and so was John. She at times was insensitive, and I think, proud, in a wrong way, and so was John. Pride and arrogance were family traits, learned from a young age and experienced at home. John at the beginning was being just like his "Mom," with pride and arrogance and a hidden agenda to be more than the other disciples, and to be closer to Jesus than all the other believers.

However, later after hearing the teachings of Jesus, and receiving his final revelation of Jesus on the Island of Patmos, John began to change and he became the pastor, the bishop, the elder, that God called him to be.

How does that apply to us and our understanding? First, we must understand that we have learned most of our behavior and personality development from our parents. They may have been the best of parents, but they may have given the worst instruction on how to deal with the problems of life. You may say, "I have always done it this way," or "my father always told me...." and you fill in the blanks. It seemed right but it may have been all wrong and it needs to change.

In John's case however, we see that one can actually change. The John of the Gospel does not seem to be the John of the epistles, in fact, some scholars have doubted that the authorship of both books as being the same. Historically, from the early church fathers, we do know that John did write both the gospel and the epistles. None the less, as explained, when John had a clear visitation of Christ in Revelation, life took on a new meaning and he had a new purpose, far beyond John's own understanding. He changed from the inside out.

One of my favorite verses in the Bible that I use regularly in counseling is I Corinthians 6:9-11. It reads,

Do you not know that the unrighteous will not inherit the kingdom of God? Do not be deceived. Neither fornicators, not idolaters, nor adulterers, nor homosexuals, nor sodomites, nor thieves, nor covetous, nor drunkards, nor revilers, nor extortioners will inherit the kingdom of God. And such were some of you. But you were washed, but you were sanctified, but you were justified in the name of the Lord Jesus and by the Spirit of God. (I Corinthians 6:9-11).

As you can see, this list shows what we once were, but we have been changed because we have been:

1. Saved; cleansed from sin.
2. We have been sanctified, which when defined, means to be "set apart" and to be made holy.

3. We are justified, which by definition means
    that we have always been sinless and right
    before God.

Sins are forgiven, men made holy, and people are made just before God and man. We are not what we once were, and we are right with God.

As we saw in Moses, in Elijah, and now in John, they all began a new relationship both with God and with man. It is as the title of the book suggests: Communion with God and Community with Man. Moses went from hostility to humility. Elijah went from depression to deliverance, and John went from arrogance to authenticity.

Authenticity is the quality of being trustworthy and genuine, and we see and feel from the Epistles of John that the writer has a pastor's heart. You sense that John really loves his people and he is authentic in his concern for their livelihood. He commands us to love over one hundred times and then he ends with a great benediction,

"But I hope to see you shortly, and we shall speak face to face. Peace to you. Our friends greet you. Greet the friends by name."
(3 John 1:14b)

John desires not to just write about it but he wants to be "authentic" and actually put it into practice by coming to visit them and show his love to all the church. We too can learn from John and not just love from a distance but go to the next step of showing love through friendship and hospitality. Hospitality always draws us into community and without it we are not being authentic in our love and compassion.

Nevertheless, we can conclude that if John can change from being arrogant to being authentic, so can we, and we can. Friends will need to be honest with us and we will need to be friendly and open with them to gain a new perspective.

Proverbs 18:24a tells us,

"A man who has friends must himself be friendly...."
(NJKV).

John learned earlier that he was a friend of God when Jesus told his disciples that,

"No longer do I call you servants, for a servant does not know what his master is doing, but I have called you friends, for all things that I heard from the Father I have made known to you." John 15:15 (NKJV).

However, he did not understand the full extent of that friendship or the friendship of believers until later, and he did not completely comprehend exactly what it meant. Later through his revelation of Jesus and with the encounters with the community of believers, he understood the commandment to "Love God and to Love Man."

Conclusion

1. It all starts with God; He initiates the relationship, the communion with God.

In my quest for simplicity and the truth of the Gospel, I started out to write a book that deals only with the basics and to explore how God is interacting with mankind to bring people into a right relationship with Him and with man. However, I also ended up exploring how in this relationship building we are building character and a stable wholeness in spiritual and mental health. In the three-character studies of Moses, Elijah, and John, in this book, I found that there was a commonality that has linked all three. It appears to me that in each incident, God first initiates the relationship with each Bible character. God comes to them, God begins the conversation, and God is the founder of the interaction. It starts with God and He is in control. All we must do is to follow his lead and then begin to respond to his reaching out to us. It has been that way from the beginning to the end of time. God the creator begins, and man follows. I think Michelangelo had it right in the famous painting of his in the Sistine Chapel in Rome for in the painting, God's finger is extended out to a deliberate point, while Adam's finger is extended downward passively responding to the initial touch of God. It is God who is making the first move with creative acts and incentives into the lives of men.

Later God in Genesis 3 is looking for Adam in the Garden of Eden, but Adam is hiding. He has broken the confidence and trust once known and established with God. Adam broke the relationship, but God is seeking to restore man from where he has fallen. God once more is being the one who starts and maintains the relationship. We see him doing that all through the Bible. Again, in the New Testament we note that God interjects himself into the lives of people. A good example of that is God's intervention into Paul's life on the road to Damascus. Paul is not seeking God, but God is seeking Paul. God is master of the plot, the writer of the script, and the author of the play that he is laying down for Paul and for us to follow. All he needs for us to do is just to begin to look and to listen and the relationship begins.

We turn now to Moses from Chapter One. Moses while tending sheep turns aside to explore the meaning of the burning bush and God speaks first and calls out to Moses, and Moses responds with a look and a listen.

Elijah as well, is in the cave depressed and again God speaks first, and Elijah turns and listens. Elijah not only listens, but he learns and is restored as he moves to correct his incorrect attributions to the events unfolding in his life.

John is taking care of business by mending his fishing nets with his brother, James, and Jesus calls him to be his disciple, and it is up to John to respond. It is God who is making the calls, setting the stage, and starting the formalities that end in a right relationship with God.

This is really a necessary concept to understand if we want to be spiritually and mentally whole for if God is the initiator, then it is up to Him to lead, not us. I do not have to take charge, and I do not have to carry the burden of making the world right and myself whole. I only have to look, listen, and learn. It is a simple task and I am not in control. He is. He provides the experience for me to enter into. Carl Jung, the famous psychologist, is his book, *"Psychology and Religion: West and East"* (1958), understood that,

One cannot just think up a system or truth which would give the patient what he needs in order to live, namely faith, hope, love and understanding. These four highest achievements of human endeavor are so many gifts of grace, which are neither to be taught nor learned, neither given or taken, neither withheld nor earned, since they come through experience, which is an irrational datum not subject to human will and caprice. Experience cannot be made. They happen...[37]

God comes to us and he is the beginning of all things good. With that first experience, God communes with us with real talk, with genuine concern, and with an understanding of who and what we are, long before we come to that same understanding. We are struggling to know how others see us, and we go to counseling to understand

---

[37] Jung, C., (1958). *Psychology and Religion: West and East*, Princeton, New Jersey: Princeton University Press, p. 331.

how we should see ourselves, but all we really need to know is how God sees us. He knew us from our mother's womb, long before we were even conscious. That gives us peace and security in the knowledge of his knowing. Our relationships are secure and firm in God and God alone, and that is fairly simple for anyone to grasp.

In our first example of Moses, we find a man, who is in a fallen state. He is angry, lost, misplaced, and "sinful." He has murdered a man, left his Hebrew family, and tries to find solace in his flight from anxiety and guilt. He is a fallen man in the same way Adam was after breaking his relationship with his creator.

But we know that God does not leave man in his fallen state, for we as Christians now know that God steps into the world through the incarnation of Jesus Christ and redeems man both past and present. Did Moses understand that at the time, I think not, but later in the New Testament while at the transfiguration of Jesus, he talks with Jesus and is a part of the renewal of all things good. When he is on the mountain in communion with God, he fully understands that Jesus as God is bringing an answer to this break in his relationship with man. God intervenes first.

In this we can come to understand Moses and his anger and…

"View human mental health and well-being in the context of God's redemptive plan. Some struggle with anger. (As seen with Moses) Others struggle with lust to the point of sexual addiction. Still others struggle to delight in their relationship with their spouse, their children, or their neighbors or co-workers. They exemplify how our mental health is not what God intends for us. They are expressions of our fallenness. Yet Christians hold out hope that God is at work redeeming these experiences and we glimpse something of our

future glory with him when we see the gains made in our mental health and well-being." [38]

As seen from the Bible and Chapter One of this book, Moses grew into a right relationship with God as God revealed himself to Moses. Then Moses with the knowledge and the spiritual and mental well-being grows into a right relationship with others. He took on a holistic approach to life and came to understand the "shalom," which is the Hebrew word that connotes justice and peace in relationships to the point of delight in them. We must delight in our Communion with God and in the Community with Man.

Elijah too responds to the initiation into God's sovereignty and answers with a positive move to correct his misconceptions of loneliness by finding a friend in Elisha. He leaves his cave and is transported

---

[38] Yarhouse, M., Butman, R., McKay, B. (2005), *Modern Psychopathologies*. Downers Grove, Illinois: Intervarsity Press.

to heaven, never to die. Later, he too on the Mount of Transfiguration, along with Moses and Jesus, comes to the knowledge of the redemption of Jesus. He sees Jesus as the God incarnate who will give his life for all of mankind.

Elijah could have stayed in the cave depressed until his death, but as in any relationship, each side responds and expresses their needs and wants, and Elijah out of his pain reached out to God. C.S. Lewis tells us that pain is the "megaphone" of God causing us to listen more carefully. God spoke and Elijah listened, and Elijah spoke, and God listened. This is remarkable for God really does listen to our cries, our prayers, and our hearts. Elijah defied God and ran from his presence, yet God gave him the freedom to do so, however, God never left. G.K. Chesterton writes,

"In making the world, He set it free. God has written, not so much a poem but rather a play; a play He had planned as perfect, but which had

necessarily been left to human actors and stage managers, who have since made a great mess of it." [39]

Yes, Elijah, at first made a mess of a victory over Baal, but God in his grace still loved Elijah so much that he took him to heaven early, to be in God's presence, even passing death's door.

And now we come to John and to the first point of God's initiative first into our lives. John is arrogant, rich (He did have a fishing business with hired hands and a house in Jerusalem), and came from a good family. Jesus approaches John where he was, there on the shores of the Sea of Galilee, and calls him into service. He calls John knowing that John has human flaws that will need to be reckoned with in the appropriate time. But again, Jesus is first on the scene and he sets the rules, rules that must be followed if the relationship is to go smoothly. John started

---

[39] Chesterton, G. (1959). *Orthodoxy*. Garden City, N.Y.: Doubleday and Company, Inc.

learning the rules but his character traits, not being like Jesus' traits, keep getting into the way. In the book, *Ego is my Enemy* (2016), the author talks of those who keep running into trouble because their **"ego decides the only way you have value is if you're better than, have more than, everyone everywhere."** [40] That is where John, "the disciple who Jesus loved," was residing in his mental and spiritual well-being. He was first with Jesus, one of the twelve, a stepson to Mary, and a man well connected. But that meant nothing to Jesus for it was God who later placed John just where he needed to be, on the Isle of Patmos. There he had a cave for a home, a rock for a pillow, and room with a view, a view to nothing. There at Jesus' initiative Jesus finishes what he started years earlier on the Sea of Galilee and John looks, listens, and learns. He is growing into that disciple that was later to be called the "apostle of love." He is learning

---

[40] Holiday, R. (2016). *Ego is the Enemy*. New York, New York: Penguin Random House Publishers. p. 117.

to have a true Communion with God and to be in Community with Man. While there on the Isle of Patmos, he not only listened to God, but he interacted with others living there and displayed the power of God through miraculous acts. Tradition will tell you that while living on the island John came into conflict with a pagan magician Kynops who is now seen to be petrified beneath the waters of the bay of Scala. John was living out the gospel now in both word and deed.

Henry Blackaby (1998) writes,

All through the Scripture, God takes the initiative. When He comes to a person, He reveals Himself and His activity. That revelation is always an invitation for the individual to adjust his life to God. None of the people God ever encountered could remain the same after the encounter. They had to make major adjustments in their lives in order to walk obediently with God.... He is the One who is the Pacesetter. He is always the One to take the initiative to accomplish what He wants to

do. When you are God-centered, even the desires to do the things that please God come from God's initiative in your life because, "it is God who works in you both to will and to do His good pleasure" (Phil. 2:13).[41]

2. If God initiates a Relationship, there must be a Response.

Moses goes from hostility to humility, Elijah transcends from depression to deliverance, and John changes from arrogance to authenticity. Once a relationship and communication are established with a fully valid revelation of God, life changes begin. 2 Corinthians 5:17 states,

---

[41] Blackaby, H., King, C. (1998). Experiencing God. Nashville, TN.: Broadman and Holman Publishers, p. 109.

'Therefore, if anyone is in Christ, he is a new creation; old things have passed away; behold all things have become new"
(NKJV).

At the initial contact with God and the burning bush, Moses, responds to the call of God with, "Here I am." Not a great act of repentance of sins and a turning away from evil, but just a simple recognition of God, Moses himself, and understanding that he, Moses, was in the presence of something outside of his own knowledge. Moses hides his face in fear and the conversation begins. This relationship must be defined and redefined over and over again as step by step God reveals himself to Moses. God does not do this just once, but time and time again and in various ways and in various places. This brings me a comfort for I too, as many of you, initially was drawn to God, but God did not allow us to stay in that comfortable place of recognition and revelation. God is constantly pushing us to new avenues of faith, fact, and familiarity. Our response is always another, "Here I am."

In the same way, Elijah too is confronted with God and as the conversation starts and the relationship defined. Elijah as well comes to a place of response and leaves the cave as commanded and begins a new mission under the leadership of God and His guidance. From Elijah's initial ministry in I Kings 17, he proceeds to go from a simple knowledge of "As the Lord, the God, of Israel lives..." to a transcendence to heaven itself as he is translated there in the fiery chariot. We never know what God is doing and when, for as in our first conclusion in paragraph one, God is in control.

John, however, is a little different in his response. At the initial call of Jesus for John to come and to leave his fishing business and follow Christ, John is constantly battling his response to God based on his own personality faults and failures. He, as Moses and Elijah, feel an inadequacy, and of course there is, but again, it is God who is in charge and all I must do is say yes to his revelation of himself to me. John's response to Christ in the Book of Revelation is similar to Moses' response in that he falls to His feet as a dead man. Christ then touches John in a way familiar with friends and with a reassurance of who He is. It is not the first time; John has felt Jesus' touch and it will not be the last as well.

What we learn from this discourse is that God is constantly revealing himself to us and touching us again and again with the understanding that His ways are not our ways. They are so majestic that we can only digest small glimpses of his revealed self.

Therefore, the second point in this discussion is that when God speaks, we must turn aside and look and listen, and then learn. And what do we learn. That is the third point in this discourse.

3. Our Response must be to follow and learn His Commands.

In our turning aside to look, we must also listen, and we then must also learn. What did Jesus teach us? What am I struggling with? What are you struggling with as well in your spiritual journey? As I wrote at the beginning of this book, I want to know, to understand, to apply my relationship with God in ways that are simple enough for my brain to comprehend. You have walked with me in this small endeavor of a book and now we have come to the end. It seemed so simple, so easy to start with the greatest command to, "Love God and Love your Neighbor," but I now see that it is only the beginning of his revelation to us.

Moses found that loving God was fairly easy, but loving the Hebrew people, who were his neighbor, was almost impossible. He finally gets it and then God upsets the "apple cart" and reveals to Moses that he also must love the "alien" living among them. Exodus 22:21 tells us,

"You shall neither mistreat a stranger (alien) nor oppress him, for you were strangers in the land of Egypt."

In the first five books of Moses we have "aliens or strangers" referenced over fifty-two times. Loving God and Loving our Neighbor has just received another manifestation.

We should have known this for the heart of God is always seeking the "sick" who need a physician. Even in the oldest book of the Bible, Job, who has gone toe to toe with God in his arguments as to his righteousness, only gets restored, when he gets it right with his neighbor. Job 42:10a says,

"And the Lord restored Job's losses when he prayed for his friends."

He was right with God, but he also had to be right with those around him. The command to Love God and Love your Neighbor sounds simple, but it is not simplistic. To have Communion with God and Community with Man sounds easy and fairly easy, and we know a little of whom God is, for he has revealed himself to us. But we must ask again, "who is our neighbor?" The Hebrew word for neighbor is, "re'a" and the first occurrence of the word comes in Genesis 11:3, at the building of the Tower of Babel, when "they said to one another (re'a)...." It has the meaning to signify all mankind that were existing at the time of the Tower of Babel. It as a generalized term meaning, "everyone" there at the time, and now when Jesus says we too must love our neighbor; we must love everyone in existence. Loving God and Loving our Neighbor sounds so simple, Communion and Community, but I again am struggling.

There is one part I forgot as I go back and read Matthew 22:37-39,

Jesus said to them, "You shall love the Lord your God with all your heart, with all your soul, and

with all your mind." "This is the first commandment." "And the second is like it, 'You shall love your neighbor as yourself." (NKJV)

I forgot that I also have to love myself. Now this one part of the verse is one that I have a difficult time in relating to, for I have been told all my life, that we must deny ourselves, but when I go back to the commandment, I think I might have found the answer. Both commandments start with love: Love God, Love Others, and Love Yourself, and one would want to say it all depends on love, but that is not true. The Bible says,

"God is love,"
(I John 4:16)

and since God is the sole proprietor of love, then it all depends on God and our relationship with Him.

As psychologist, theologians, medical doctors, and philosophers have all told us: "Human beings were made to delight in relationship with God, themselves, each other and the rest of creation." [42]

So, what is the conclusion? Solomon tells us;

"Let us hear the conclusion of the whole matter: Fear God and keep His commandments, For this is Man's all."
(Ecc. 12:13).

And what did Jesus say was the command, "Love God, Love your Neighbor, and Love Yourself.

Communion with God, Community with Man, and Communion with Ourselves. I think I might be a little closer to the answer that I have been seeking. It really is a God thing and nothing more. All of my relationships depend on His love for me and with

---

[42] Yarhouse, M., Butman, R., McKay, B. (2005), *Modern Psychopathologies*. Downers Grove, Illinois: Intervarsity Press.

that love, I begin to love as well. Simple, maybe, but not simplistic for sure.

To close this book, let me quotes I John 3:2,

"Beloved , new we are the children of God, and it has not yet been revealed what we shall be, but we know that when He is revealed, we shall be like Him, for we shall see Him as He is.(NKJV).

In each example that we have looked at, each person, each believer, they all had an initial revelation of God, but there was more to come, more revelations followed. I want you to ask God to continue to reveal Himself more and more to you, so that you may become like Him. Today, open your heart and look, listen, and learn. There is still more to come.

Bibliography

Baab, O. (1949). *The Theology of the Old Testament*. New York, New York: Abingdon/Cokesbury.

Babuata, L. *Quote on Simplicity*. Leobabuata.com.

Baker, J. (2000). *The Refuge*. Nashville, TN.: Thomas Nelson Publishers.

Beaumont, M. (2012). *The New Lion Bible Encyclopedia*. Oxford, England: Lion Hudson Publishers.

Blackaby, H., King, C. (1998). Experiencing God. Nashville, TN.: Broadman and Holman Publishers.

Bonhoeffer, D. (1954). *Life Together*. New York, New York: HarperCollins Publishers.

Brown, R. (1984). *The Churches the Apostles Left Behind*. Mahwah, New Jersey: Paulist Press.

Caird, G. (1966). *A Commentary of The Revelation of St. John the Divine.* New York, NY.: Harper and Row Publishers, p. 25.

Camci, M. *Ephesus.* Istanbul, Turkey: Alas Ticaret ve Basim Sanayi

Chesterton, G. (1959). *Orthodoxy.* Garden City, N.Y.: Doubleday and Company, Inc.

Dominus et Deus: see Dio Cassius lxvii. 13; Suetonius, *Dom.* 13; Martial v.8.

Eastman, D. (2012). *Look What God is Doing.* Colorado Springs, Colorado: Every Home for Christ.

Friedman, R. (2017). *The Exodus.* New York, New York: Harper One Publishers.

Hafner, A. (2002). *Anger.* Center City, Mn.: Hazelden Press.

Holiday, R. (2016). *Ego is the Enemy.* New York, New York: Penguin Random House Publishers.

Ingersoll, B., Goldstein, S. (1995*). Lonely, Sad, and Angry, A Parent's Guide to Depression in Children* *and Adolescents*. New York, New York: Doubleday.

Jeremiah, D. (2013). *The Jeremiah Study Bible.* Nashville, TN.: Worthy Publishing.

Jung, C., (1958). *Psychology and Religion: West and East*, Princeton, New Jersey: Princeton University Press, p. 331.

Kelly-Gangi. (2006). *Mother Teresa Her Essential Wisdom*. New York, New York: Falls River Press.

Kushner, H. (1981). *When Bad Things Happen to Good People*. New York, New York: Anchor Books.

Kushner, H. (1986). *When All You've Ever Wanted Isn't Enough*. New York, New York: Summit Books.

Kidder, D., Oppenheim, N. (2006). *The Intellectual Devotional*. New York, New York: Rodale.

Martin, R. (2006) *The Fulfillment of all Desire*. Steubenville, Ohio: Emmaus Road Publishing.

Martin, W. (1964). *The Layman's Bible Encyclopedia.* Nashville, Tn.: The Southwestern Company.

McBirnie, W. (1977). *The Search for the Twelve Apostles.* Wheaton, Illinois: Tyndale Publishing House.

Meier, P., Minirth, F., Wichern, F. (1982). *Introduction to Psychology and Counseling.* Grand Rapids, Michigan: Baker Book House.

Morris, W. (1976). *The American Heritage Dictionary of the English Language.* Boston, Mass.: Houghton Mifflin Company.

Stowell, J. (2020). *Seven Churches of Revelation.* Day of Discovery Television Series.

Szasz, T. (1974). *The Myth of Mental Illness.* New York, New York: Harper and Row Publishers.

Tenney, M. (1963). *The Zondervan Pictorial Bible Dictionary.* Grand Rapids, Michigan: Zondervan Publishing House.

Teresa of Avila, *The Interior Castle.* Sect. I, Chap. 2, no. 9.

The Holy Bible, New King James Version (1982). Nashville, TN.: Thomas Nelson Publishers.

Vitz, P. (1977). *Psychology as Religion, The Cult of Self-Worship*. Grand Rapids, Michigan: William B. Eerdmans Publishing Company.

Warren, R. (2006). *God's Answers to Life's Difficult Questions*. Grand Rapids, MI.: Zondervan.

Yarhouse, M., Butman, R., McKay, B. (2005), *Modern Psychopathologies*. Downers Grove, Illinois: Intervarsity Press.

Zodhiades, S. (1990). *The Hebrew- Greek Key Study Bible*. Chattanooga, TN.: AMG Publishers.

End Notes

Scripture quotations marked (NKJV) are taken from the New King James Version of the Bible, copyright 1982 by Thomas Nelson, Inc., Nashville, Tennessee, USA. Used by permission. All rights reserved.

All pictures used were from Public Domain except otherwise noted:

From Unsplash.com

Page 27:

Mt. Sinai – Vlad-Kiselov-Fe3e F795054-unsplash

Page 53:

Book of Ephesus – sincerely-media-x ObwQCSW8O-unsplash

Library Façade of Ephesus – jennifer-martin-x JKkpD3F3tX4-unsplash

Additional Books by the Author:

Tilley, A. (2018) *The 38 Days of Christmas Devotional,* *Columbia,* South Carolina: Kindle Direct Publishing/Amazon Books.

Tilley, A. (2018) *A History and Guide to Biblical Sites in* *Cyprus,* CreateSpace/Amazon Books.

Tilley, A. (2020) *Finding Christ in Muslim Lands,* Kindle Direct Publishing/Amazon Books.

www.ingramcontent.com/pod-product-compliance
Lightning Source LLC
Chambersburg PA
CBHW051447250726
48655CB00001B/292